J K Rowling

the mystery of fiction

[an unauthorised biography]

Lindsey Fraser

ARGYLL ✤ PUBLISHING

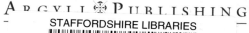

© Lindsey Fraser 2011

Argyll Publishing
Glendaruel
Argyll PA22 3AE
Scotland

www.argyllpublishing.co.uk

The author has asserted
her moral rights.

**British Library
Cataloguing-in-
Publication Data.
A catalogue record for
this book is available
from the British Library.**

ISBN 978 1 906134 69 3

ALBA | CHRUTHACHAIL

Printing:
Martins the Printers,
Berwick upon Tweed

CONTENTS

ACKNOWLEDGEMENTS

Many thanks to Kathryn Ross and The Gifford
Safe Haven, to Grainne Ballantyne (neé Cooney),
Jane Churchill, Robert and Patrick Fraser,
Alyx Price, Fraser Smith, Janet Smyth,
Imogen Wilkinson, Sarah Wright and all those who
talked with me about what the words 'Harry' and
'Potter' triggered in their brains.

PREFACE

WHO hasn't heard of Harry Potter? You may never have read the books, but the chances are you've seen one of the films, munched a handful of Bertie Bott's Every Flavour Beans or played Harry Potter Top Trumps with your friends.

The seven novels and three related books by J K Rowling have resulted in a worldwide media phenomenon which includes translations of the books throughout the world, films, merchandise, food, toys, games, a Florida theme park, and a vast online community of fans, including writers of fan fiction who take the characters and the settings and launch them into a whole new range of adventures. And that phenomenon continues to expand. As long as there are new ways developed for us to entertain ourselves, Harry Potter and his friends will play their part.

That extraordinary story began with a book for children written by an author who had remarkable ambition and drive. Today J K Rowling's Harry Potter novels are available in 69 languages throughout the world, including Welsh, Irish, Latin and Ancient Greek. It's a tally that can only increase.

Harry Potter is a one-off.

There will be many splendid books written for young people in the future, but Harry Potter had a unique momentum – driven by the children who first read the books, followed swiftly by business executives who knew a magical opportunity when they saw one.

Back in 1997, when Joanne Rowling's first novel was published, nobody could have predicted the popularity of *Harry Potter and the Philosopher's Stone*, or what happened next.

The author admits that she privately believed that if she found a publisher, her books could be very successful. But even in her wildest dreams, Jo Rowling could not then have imagined just how successful. Within a few years, Hollywood directors would be beating a path to her door requesting her sketches, explanations and illustrations, and samples of merchandising – from Harry Potter spectacle frames to Hogwarts scarves to Harry Potter wands and even Moaning Myrtle lavatory seat alarms – would be arriving for her approval (or disapproval). Theme park designers from Universal Orlando Resort would be showing her diagrams of the town of Hogmeades™, plans for Ollivanders™, 'makers of fine wands since 382BC', and the popular Zonko's™ joke shop, and testing recipes for Butterbeer™, the vanilla-flavoured drink which now refreshes visitors to The Wizarding World of Harry Potter™.

Jo Rowling has remained at the heart of all these developments and activities. Everybody involved in taking the world of Harry Potter beyond the pages of the books had to pay close attention to her. She knows everything there is to know about that world and the characters who populate it. It is her world and they are her characters, and if anybody were to take non-Potter-like liberties with either, they would alienate her millions of readers and torpedo their potential market.

This book tells the story of the author, J K Rowling, and her books, how the publishing and bookselling worlds stepped up to the bar – even when that bar kept being raised, how readers responded to the unfolding story, and how the landscape for children's books has altered as a result of an idea that popped into somebody's head one day on a train from Manchester to London.

CHAPTER ONE

What if. . .?

EVERYONE'S life is made up of stories of one kind or another. We choose our friends because their stories appeal to us. What music do they listen to? What do they read? How do they spend their spare time? What have we in common? What are their politics? Nobody has total control – for example, we can't choose our parents – but every day we make choices which influence how the next chapter in our lives unfolds, choices based on answers to the all-important 'What if?' questions. What if I take this subject next year at school? What if I buy this laptop? What if I make friends with that crowd? What if I choose to read this book instead of revising for my exams?

That 'What if?' question is central to the life of a writer too. What if I take what I know and give it a twist? What if I make it comic? A horror story? A fantasy? What if I set it in the here-and-now? The there-and-then? Another planet? Whether an author starts with a character, a setting, an idea or an opening sentence, their task is then to make the many decisions which drive their story on to its conclusion. They need to hold our interest, or we may stop turning the pages and turn out the light. . .

Every writer, published and unpublished, has a different way of working. It's a profession well known for specific demands and routines. But wherever they live and whatever implements they use, writers write and they write and they write. Then they read what they've written, they check and edit, they re-read the revised version, they re-edit it, and then they continue to write and edit until finally they read what they've written and they decide, 'It's ready. It tells the story I want to tell.'

J K Rowling has her own routines and preferences. She likes to write her stories in longhand in cafés and she makes copious notes, drawings and diagrams. She has said that because she didn't have a pen and paper with her on the train journey from Manchester during which the idea for Harry Potter eased its way into her imagination, the plot established itself very clearly.

'I have never felt such a huge rush of excitement. I knew *immediately* that this was going to be such fun to write.'

By the time she got off the train in London she had

established the structure for her seven novels, several characters and much of the Hogwarts timetable – the ideas had flooded her imagination, all ready to be written. After several false starts, she finally began to write the story that would make her famous.

Jo Rowling remembers writing her first book when she was six. She admits that it was a rip-off of the Richard Scarry books that she loved: it was about a rabbit called Rabbit, and she remembers wanting it to be published. 'I wanted the complete experience, even then.' She was an enthusiastic reader, particularly encouraged by her mother, Anne, who loved books.

Anne and Peter Rowling were young parents. They had met and fallen in love on the train from King's Cross Station in London to Arbroath where they were to be posted – they were in the navy at the time. They were both 20 when Joanne was born on July 31, 1965, and two years later, they had a second daughter, Dianne.

When she was four, Jo's family moved from Chipping Sodbury, just north of Bristol where she had been born, to the village of Winterbourne, on the outskirts of Bristol, where she went to school for the first time. The family then moved to Tutshill near Chepstow in Wales, on the River Wye, when Jo was nine. Their house there had originally been the village school, next to the church with its graveyard.

Jo wasn't nearly as happy at school in Tutshill as she had been in Winterbourne. It was a much more old-fashioned establishment and she observed in some of her teachers a liking for the power they could exert over their pupils. She knuckled down in order to master the rote learning necessary to pass the regular tests, and gradually she settled in.

The house in Tutshill was the picture postcard home her parents had dreamed of for their young family, an easy commute for her father to the Rolls Royce factory where he was an engineer. Jo recalls happy times when she wasn't at school. She and her sister enjoyed heading out to nearby Offa's Dyke, the Anglo Saxon earthen wall put up by King Offa, the King of Mercia, to keep the marauding Welsh out of his kingdom. 'We used to love exploring amongst the boulders,' she once said. The graveyard, despite their friends' anxieties, was another favourite place. 'I still love graveyards – they are a great source of names.'

Secondary school for Jo and Di was Wyedean School, where their mother worked as a technician in the science labs. It was there that Jo was taught by Miss Shepherd, a firm but fair English teacher for whom she had enormous respect. Miss Shepherd taught Jo about the structure and discipline of writing, and encouraged her to read widely. 'She was the only teacher I ever confided in,' Rowling says. 'She inspired trust.'

Otherwise, Jo loved art, loathed hockey, and quite enjoyed gym. She is particularly scathing about her abilities in the woodwork and metalwork class. 'I am *not* a practical person. . .'

Jo has described herself as 'a tiny bit Hermione-ish' at secondary school, very keen to please and get things right, and a great worrier. 'I think I was always very insecure. . . but I would put on a show of confidence to mask it.'

Jo was 12 when her mother first began to show symptoms of Multiple Sclerosis, a complex and unpredictable disease which affects the central nervous system. It took some years before the official diagnosis was given, and because Anne Rowling had a particularly aggressive form of the illness, her mobility and motor functions were badly affected at a tragically young age.

Jo's affection for her mother and her devastation at the ordeal of her illness and her early death remain a very present element in the writer's life.

Being a teenager in a country village can be limiting, but there were always books. Jo was a precocious and voracious reader, fortunate in having lots of her parents' books from which to choose. But when a great aunt gave her *Hons and Rebels* by Jessica Mitford when she was in her mid-teens, she was captivated. Jessica Mitford's autobiography is witty and insightful, the story of a girl brought up in a smothering if entertaining household, and her bid for escape – running away with Winston Churchill's nephew to fight in the Spanish Civil War.

Jo was particularly impressed by the fact that Jessica bought a camera for the trip, boldly charging it to her father's account. 'I wish I'd had the nerve to do something like that,' she says. But it was Jessica Mitford's commitment to socialism and human rights throughout her life which so appealed to the teenage Jo Rowling. 'I love the way she never outgrew some of her adolescent traits, remaining true to her politics. I think I've read everything she wrote. I even called my daughter after her.'

When she was in the Upper Sixth Form and head girl, a new pupil, Sean Harris, arrived at school. Or to be more precise, Sean Harris and his turquoise Ford Anglia arrived at school. The car and its driver spelt freedom for Jo at a time when family life must have been very tough indeed. That turquoise Ford Anglia was to turn up for a dramatic rescue mission in the second of Jo's Harry Potter novels, just as it rescued her when she needed it most.

When she left school, Jo went to Exeter University, a short drive from Tutshill. She had always wanted to study English, believing that if she wanted to be a writer, that would be the most appropriate course. But she was under some pressure to take a course which would more clearly lead to a job, so she accepted a place to read Modern Languages. However, having waved her parents farewell, Jo had already decided that they weren't getting it all their own way. 'Hardly had my parents' car rounded the corner at the end of the road than I ditched German and scuttled off down the Classics corridor,' she admitted to Harvard graduates some years later.

Jo had the best of both worlds. She was now studying at least one subject she enjoyed and she was entitled to spend a year in Paris. Her university career wasn't one of unadulterated excellence. She admits that she spent much of her time writing stories when she should have been attending lectures and that she was fortunate in having 'a knack for passing examinations'. But she made many good friends whose support and loyalty would prove invaluable in years to come.

Once she had graduated, Jo went to London where she trained as a bi-lingual secretary. She has been extremely rude about her abilities as a secretary, but she learned to type and although she has expressed some misgivings about her career moves at the time, that skill has been central to her life as a writer. She worked for a time for Amnesty International – 'If I wasn't writing full time it was important that my time was spent on something worthwhile' – and then moved to Manchester with her then boyfriend.

But not long after that, at the end of 1990, Jo's mother died aged 45. Although the outcome of her mother's illness had been inevitable, the loss was utterly shocking and it threw Jo into a period of desperate misery. She was made redundant, then found another job but she couldn't settle. In the end, she decided that the best thing would be for her to move completely away and she went to live in Portugal, earning her living by teaching English as a foreign language.

Jo took with her copious quantities of paper on which were written the notes for an idea she had had six months before her mother's death. It was while she had been on a train from Manchester to London that the idea for Harry Potter had entered her mind.

What if. . . there was a boy who didn't know that he was a wizard? Unusually she had no pen or paper on the journey. All she could do was to accept this rush of ideas and stories that were cascading into her imagination, make them her own, and then write them down the minute she arrived home.

'By the end of that train journey I knew it was going to be a seven-book series,' she said. 'I know that's extraordinarily arrogant for somebody who had never been published but that's how it came to me.'

Jo enjoyed her teaching in Portugal. Most of her pupils were in their mid to late teens, an age-group she found engaging and stimulating. Her timetable had enough space in it for her to write, to work on the detailed plan for her series of books about the boy wizard. During that time Jo met and married Jorge Arantes, a Portuguese journalist with whom she had her first daughter, Jessica. But the relationship was an unhappy one, and at the end of November 1993, just over a year after they had married, Jo left.

The decision to leave Portugal had been swift and difficult and Jo had made no preparations, arriving in a wintry Edinburgh with a three-month-old baby. She had brought only what she could carry and she had absolutely no idea what she was going to do in order to support herself and her daughter.

Jo chose to come to Edinburgh because her sister Di, a lawyer, lived in the city. It was a sensible decision but nothing prepared her for how life was to be. The reality of being a single mother claiming benefits was shattering. The turbulent months in which she had taken the decision to leave her marriage and Portugal were behind her and when she finally came to a halt, Jo began to suffer from depression.

She has described it as 'characterised by a numbness and a coldness and an inability to believe you will feel happy again. All the colour drained out of life.' She experienced acute anxiety attacks that the one good thing she had – her baby – would be taken from her. Depression is an illness which strikes people in different ways. But common to any depression is the need to work hard to break free from it. Depression rarely fades without huge effort on the part of the sufferer.

Despite her parlous situation, Jo was fortunate. She had a degree, she had considerable work experience, and she had the motivation – her daughter – to pull herself out of the pit of gloom in which she was living. A friend helped fund her through a teaching qualification, and although she and Jessica were a long way from being either financially secure or settled into the kind of home she wanted for them both, that qualification provided the route out of her misery. It began to restore Jo's confidence. There was a future for them after all.

But always, in notebooks and in her head, there was Harry Potter. She could not leave the idea alone, and it would not leave her.

By 1994, Joanne Rowling was working hard towards establishing a teaching career that would provide a regular income as she and her daughter settled into a new life in a new city. But her passion for stories gnawed away at her. She wanted to give herself a chance to do what she had always dreamed of doing – writing a novel. One day she asked herself, 'What if I take the one thing I believe I can do, and write the book that I've always wanted to write?' She felt she had nothing to lose.

Back then she was like many other aspiring writers. She snatched every available opportunity to write, using the walk from her flat to the coffee shop in which she enjoyed writing to send Jessica to sleep, making the most of her daughter's nap to work further on her novel, writing into the night once the baby was in her bed.

Now, having published ten books, J K Rowling is not like many other writers. Her novels have sold in quantities previously unknown in the world of books for young people, her stories form the basis of a global brand, her personal and professional life has changed completely and she is wealthy beyond the dreams of most individuals.

During the years since 1994, Joanne Rowling has become J K Rowling.

Harry Potter has become a household name.

People everywhere have been witness to a powerful global literary and media phenomenon.

The world has gained a gutsy philanthropist.

CHAPTER TWO

Breaking news

O N 24th June 1997, *The Herald*, one of Scotland's main newspapers, ran an article written by the journalist Anne Johnstone in which she introduced a new Edinburgh-based writer, Joanne Rowling. The piece was timed to coincide with the publication by Bloomsbury Children's Books of Joanne's début novel, *Harry Potter and the Philosopher's Stone*. The interview had taken place in Nicolson's, a popular café on Edinburgh's South Bridge where, Joanne explained, she had spent many hours writing her book.

In the interview, Joanne spoke frankly about the difficult circumstances in which she found herself living as a single parent with a baby after she came to live in Edinburgh in 1994. She talked about the importance of the book she'd written and of writing in helping her through some dark days. 'The book saved my sanity,' she told Anne Johnstone. 'Apart from my sister I knew nobody (in Edinburgh). I'd never been more broke and the little I had went on baby gear. In the wake of my marriage, having worked all my life, I was suddenly an unemployed single parent in a grotty little flat. The manuscript was the only thing I had going for me.'

Anne Johnstone couldn't have known then that she was interviewing the author of what was to become the world's most successful series of books for children, and all that accompanied it. But there are indications that she was aware this début wasn't just a run-of-the-mill children's book. She reported on an ongoing auction amongst American publishers for the right to publish Joanne's book in America. This was unusual in the world of children's books – and there were signs of an outcome involving a sum of dollars that was equally unusual. She drew comparisons between Joanne's writing and that of another best-selling children's writer. 'Harry is completely believable and redolent of various Roald Dahl characters, especially Charlie Bucket and Matilda,' she said. And in a prescient aside, she envisaged possibilities for future film adaptations. 'The cinematic effects which brought the latter to life could do the same for Potter,' she suggested.

There were a remarkable number of similar articles published that summer considering that this was a first time author of a novel for young people. The staff in the publicity department at Bloomsbury Children's Books had done an excellent job. As a result of their enthusiasm and probably some polite pestering, many national newspapers had taken up the story of the penniless single mother and her overnight writing success.

At the time, I was working for Scottish Book Trust, an organisation which encourages people of all ages to read for pleasure. Many of my days were spent talking to children, teachers, parents and librarians, recommending books I thought they would enjoy too. I was also an occasional children's book reviewer for *The Scotsman* newspaper and in the edition published on June 28th, 1997, I sang the praises of *Harry Potter and the Philosopher's Stone*. There was never any shortage of good children's books to write about, but in the mid-1990s I was not alone in wearying a bit of gritty realism – the kind of book in which an 'issue' – the grimmer the better – came galloping over the horizon at speed. Dysfunctional families, bullies and the bullied, death and bereavement – the trend was for books reflecting 'real' life. *Harry Potter and the Philosopher's Stone* made a refreshing and enjoyable change. Although looking back, the series has since proved full of dysfunctional families, bullies and the bullied, death and bereavement.

We selected J K Rowling's first novel for Scottish Book Trust's annual summer reading campaign. Supporting and promoting authors living in Scotland was an important part of our remit, and we were delighted to add *Harry* to an already excellent list. Librarians throughout Scotland bought multiple copies of the books included in these campaigns for their libraries, so publishers were naturally enthusiastic about having their books included. I recall that Rosamund Walker (now Rosamund de la Hey), who was then organising the publicity and marketing for Bloomsbury Children's Books, went to considerable trouble to send us an early image of the jacket of *Harry Potter and the Philosopher's Stone* so that we could meet our print deadline and include it on the Now Read On posters and bookmarks.

It was Rosamund who had alerted us to the book earlier that year when she sent us the manuscript. This wasn't unusual. The best possible way to promote a book for young people is to ensure that everybody is talking about it so Rosamund sent copies of the manuscript to people involved with enthusing young people about books, people she knew would tell other people about it. She even included a packet of sweets in some of the parcels – a smart way of making sure recipients paid attention.

It isn't unusual for publicists to sound enthusiastic about the books they are promoting, but sometimes it becomes obvious that they've read little more than the blurb on the back jacket. Rosamund was not like that. I remember her phoning a few days later to check that we had received the manuscript. We had, and I'd just started reading it.

I told her I was already enjoying it – I had been particularly amused by the idea of the Put-Outer that Albus Dumbledore uses to extinguish the street lights – and promised to let her know what I thought when I had finished. We all enjoyed reading it, delighted to have a new book to tell readers about, delighted too, to be able to support a local author. I sent Rosamund an enthusiastic quote for her to use as she saw fit and assured her that we would do all we could to help Joanne Rowling on her way. In retrospect that offer seems spectacularly naive.

News of this new children's book was spreading in the book trade. Sarah Wright was, and continues to be a publisher's rep. Her job is to visit bookshops and to encourage their buyers to order her range of books. The more books they stock the better the publishers she represents like it. Sarah is a lively character, direct and no-nonsense. She doesn't simply flip over the pages of her catalogues – she's the sort of rep who thinks about what's going to suit each individual customer. As a result, her appointments are more like conversations between friends than selling sessions.

In 1997 Sarah was representing books published by one of the UK's biggest publishers and she remembers that the children's book buyers in the shops she visited would often tell her about this début novel by an Edinburgh author, *Harry Potter and the Philosopher's Stone*. 'I remember one Waterstone's buyer holding up the proof and telling me this was going to be the summer's big book. There are always opinions about books on the go, books that people get all excited about. That doesn't necessarily mean they'll be bestsellers, but there was something a bit different about this one.'

Sarah mentioned the buzz surrounding the book in one of the regular reports she wrote for her boss. 'It's good for publishers to know what other publishers are doing, and I often mentioned the competition.' But on that occasion her boss didn't take her very seriously, and in the general report that was compiled from those of all her colleagues throughout the country, Sarah's mention of Harry Potter was edited out. 'Children's books just weren't seen as important back then,' Sarah says. 'They sold well, but they didn't make news and they weren't expected to sell in really big numbers.'

Sarah remembers a conversation a few months later with a senior editor in her publishing house. 'She was disappointed that I hadn't told them about Harry. She felt I should have known about it as I was based in Edinburgh. I tried to explain that I had, that the information had been left out of the general report. I think she was exasperated by the regular criticism the big publishers were getting for having missed out on the Harry Potter book.'

There must have been many editors who, during the autumn of 1997, couldn't help checking their records. Had they been one of those who had turned down that unsolicited submission from the unknown author from Edinburgh, Joanne Rowling? The book that everybody was talking about?

CHAPTER THREE

Good contacts

JOANNE Rowling had originally submitted her novel to a few publishers herself. Like so many aspiring writers before her, she had gone to her local library and found listings of publishers in the *Writers' and Artists' Yearbook*, a wonderful compendium of information for writers.

Jo didn't have a computer at the time and she had ended up typing the manuscript twice. Her training as a touch typist now proved very useful. She was concerned that the word count was higher than most children's books being published at that time, so she typed it in single spacing so that it took up fewer pages to disguise the length. But when she discovered that publishers prefer double-spaced submissions because they are less dense to read, she retyped the whole thing.

Because photocopying the complete manuscript was so expensive, and money was tight, Jo submitted it to one publisher at a time, enduring – as most authors have to – the nail-biting wait while the publisher considers it, decides against it, and then returns the manuscript in the stamped addressed envelope supplied by the author. If they're lucky. Then they have to pick themselves up, dust themselves down and the whole cycle begins again. Finding a publisher is rarely a speedy process.

Brown envelopes containing would-be writers' hopes and dreams are part of the daily ritual of working in a publishing house. There are far more manuscripts submitted than there are books published. Today, because publishers tend to have fewer staff than they had, most of them stipulate that submissions can only be made via a Literary Agent – somebody who represents individual writers' interests, hoping to secure the right publisher, and broker the publishing contract which is the happy outcome of which all writers dream. So most writers start by finding themselves a Literary Agent.

In 1995, Jo successfully approached the Christopher Little Literary Agency – more photocopying and another set of stamps and return postage – and it was with their enthusiastic support that her manuscript finally landed on the desk of Barry Cunningham, who was then in charge of publishing books for young people at Bloomsbury Children's Books.

In many ways Barry Cunningham was the perfect person to launch Jo Rowling's career as a novelist. He now has his own publishing company – Chicken House – but in the early 1990s he had launched the children's list for Bloomsbury Publishing plc, then a relatively new independent publisher.

Bloomsbury had been established in 1986 by Nigel Newton, an energetic American who had worked for several publishers before starting his own company. Naturally the headquarters of the company are in Bloomsbury, a fashionable part of central London. But the name also relates to the Bloomsbury Set, a group of writers, artists and intellectuals who provided a running commentary on the arts, society and culture for much of the first part of the twentieth century.

Virginia Woolf, Vanessa Bell, Lytton Strachey and E M Forster were amongst the famous names who met regularly, who wrote, debated, argued, designed and painted, providing a fascinating interpretation of a period of great social and political upheaval in Britain. Nowadays there would probably be a Bloomsbury Set blog, a website, lots of tweeting and possibly even podcasts, but in those pre-internet days, meetings, exhibitions, talks and articles were an effective way of making people sit up and take note.

In the early days Bloomsbury Publishing plc specialised in literary fiction for adults, publishing such authors as Margaret Atwood, Jay McInerney, Donna Tartt and Michael Ondaatje, outstanding writers whose books always provoke debate and discussion amongst critics and readers. The original titles were printed on high quality paper, with ribbon markers and elegantly designed jackets. Today most Bloomsbury books are less extravagant, but the company still retains a tradition of publishing stylish special editions of some of their classic bestsellers alongside the general hardbacks and paperbacks. That expertise would come in handy for the Harry Potter books.

By the early 1990s, publishing for children had gone through a quiet revolution and it made sense for Bloomsbury, having enjoyed considerable commercial success as a publisher of books for adults, to venture into that market. Until the end of the 1970s, almost every children's book had been published first in hardback by a publisher that specialised in publishing hardback books. The paperback edition would then appear a year or so later, published by a different publisher that specialised in paperbacks.

Hamish Hamilton published E B White's *Charlotte's Web*, Joan Lingard's *Twelfth Day of July* and Eric Carle's *The Very Hungry Caterpillar* in hardback, but the paperback editions were published by Puffin Books. Oxford University Press published Rosemary Sutcliffe,

Geraldine MacCaughrean and Philippa Pearce in hard-back, but their paperbacks were published by Puffin Books. Collins published C S Lewis's *Narnia* series in hardback, but again, the paperback editions were published by Puffin Books. Jonathan Cape published Roald Dahl's hardbacks, and yet again Puffin was in charge of the paperbacks.

In the early 1980s, several publishers decided to rethink the traditional pattern of publishing for young people. Why not control the publication of books in hardback *and* paperback, rather than find them and then farm them out elsewhere to be published in paperback? It made good commercial and creative sense. As a result, many smaller independent publishers, partic-ularly those who were famous for their hardback publishing, were bought up by bigger companies who wanted the paperback rights to their famous backlists.

An example of this kind of acquisition was Penguin's purchase of Frederick Warne and Co, Beatrix Potter's publisher. She was the famous author and illustrator of twenty-three little books, the first of which was published in 1902 – *The Story of Peter Rabbit*. But she was also enterprising and entrepreneurial. She had originally self-published her first book, but once she was working with a publisher, she took great pleasure in overseeing the merchandising – dolls, china tea sets and board games. No author for children had ever done this before.

some of the bigger publishing houses. But perhaps his decision was more strategic than financial.

After all, Jo Rowling was an unknown. Her book wasn't an obvious bestseller; indeed in some ways it might have been viewed as old-fashioned, with its boarding school setting, orphaned hero and magical adventures. But because the Bloomsbury list was still quite small she would be a bigger fish in a smaller pond than she might have been with Puffin or Collins. The Bloomsbury team would have more time and energy to spend launching and promoting *Harry Potter and the Philosopher's Stone* than staff at bigger publishers who had responsibility for a greater number of titles, and better-known authors. So it may have been more of a necessity than a gamble, but in the end Christopher Little's decision to send the manuscript to Bloomsbury and his recommendation that his client accept their modest offer for her first book was a good one.

Barry has never claimed that his decision to make that offer reflected anything other than an immediate enthusiasm. He says he wasn't aware that it had been submitted to quite a number of publishers by the time it reached him. He simply read and enjoyed it. Interviewed by *Fortune Magazine* in 2006 he said, 'I just knew it was a great book. . . I think everybody else passed on it for all the wrong reasons. It was long, the title was unusual and the story is pretty dark. Rowling needed someone to see what it was, a story of bravery and danger and adventure but with great humour – as opposed to what it wasn't, a traditional children's book.'

Whatever it was that persuaded Barry Cunningham to make an offer for *Harry Potter and the Philosopher's Stone* in the autumn of 1996, his decision led to publishing history being made. Not that he or anybody else had any inkling of what the future held.

Jo was ecstatic. Very belatedly, another major publisher entered the frame but she decided not to negotiate any further. She was thrilled to have been made the offer by Bloomsbury and appreciated their early enthusiasm. Barry took Jo out to lunch once his offer had been accepted and firmly told her not to give up the day job which was, at that point, teaching French part-time at Leith Academy, an Edinburgh secondary school.

Very few authors earn a lot of money from their books, not even those who have been published many times over a long period. Anne Fine once famously said that most authors earn less than peanuts. So Barry's was sensible advice, advice any writer should be given in the heady aftermath of their first offer of a contract.

Back in the office however, he was talking the book up to colleagues, creating the in-house buzz which propelled *Harry Potter and the Philosopher's Stone* beyond Bloomsbury's Soho Square HQ and into the book trade's consciousness in a way few children's books had done before. Certainly not first novels.

Rosamund de la Hey was on the case with him, spreading the word, talking to booksellers, drumming up press coverage, and convincing everybody she could that this was a book with a bright future. Copies of the manuscript were circulated, proofs printed and sent out, and positive feedback flowed in. Rosamund had never had such a strong reaction to a book.

CHAPTER FIVE

Opening chapters

To understand how the economic success surrounding J K Rowling's novels began, it's useful to understand a little about how publishing works. This is the business end of what usually happens after a publisher agrees to publish a book.

The publisher offers the author a sum of money when they accept a book for publication. That sum of money is called an advance. Usually, an advance is paid to the author in thirds – the first once the contract has been signed, the second when the manuscript is completed and delivered to the publisher's satisfaction, and the third once the book is published and on sale in bookshops. The advance is a bit like a loan from a publisher, but not one that has to be paid back, unless in exceptional circumstances.

Every publisher hopes to recoup the advance they've

paid to the author through healthy sales of the book. And they hope to keep earning money by selling copies of the book for as long as possible.

After a book has been published, it starts to earn back the publisher's advance. Every time a book is sold in bookshops, or to libraries and book clubs, the author is entitled to receive a very small percentage of each book's sale price – called a royalty. The royalties accumulate with the publisher and gradually, if things go according to plan, these little bits of money add up until the royalties equal the sum of money paid by the publisher in the advance. This is called 'earning out'. After the advance has been 'earned out' (or paid off) the royalties are paid by the publisher to the author, usually twice a year.

Other earnings go towards helping to 'earn out' the advance. Foreign rights are bought by publishers to allow them to translate the book to sell in their country. Every spring there is a big book fair in Bologna in Italy attended by publishers and literary agents specialising in children's books from all over the world. The more foreign rights they sell, the more income the book generates, and the more the author, the literary agent and the publisher earns.

Every new set of rights sold is a potential source of income – for audio books, for extracts for magazines, for tv and film, for dramatisation. As long as the author holds the copyright for their book, no part of it can be used without their permission. Today digital rights are important – the development of e-readers and smart phones and the ability to download books easily opens up a whole new range of rights to buy and sell and ways to read books too. With technology bounding ahead, publishers have to run to keep up with the possibilities. But however exotic or inventive the options are, they all refer back to that original manuscript, the words on the page.

An offer of the kind that Jo Rowling accepted from Bloomsbury for her first novel may sound like a triumphant final step for an author, but in fact it can be the beginning of a whole new story. Assuming things go well.

In the case of *Harry Potter and the Philosopher's Stone*, Jo's literary agent sold Bloomsbury the right to publish and sell the book in the UK and certain other countries including the Republic of Ireland, Australia, New Zealand and South Africa. The alternative would have been for Bloomsbury to have bought world rights to the book – buying the author's permission to sell the rights themselves. This is what most publishers prefer.

But the Christopher Little Literary Agency retained the rights to Jo's novel in other countries and languages, taking on that responsibility itself. And right from the start, they sought foreign publishers. Jane Churchill, Director of the Children's Programme at the Cheltenham Literary Festival, also works for Gallimard, one of France's most prestigious and innovative publishers. She recalls receiving an early proof of *Harry Potter and the Philosopher's Stone* and recommending it as a book Gallimard should seriously consider. 'I was very keen on it from the start,' Jane says, 'but it was very different for the Gallimard list, very different for France too, and it took the editors a while to decide to translate it. They were hesitant about committing themselves to such a long series of books, I suppose. But in the end they took the plunge, and the Harry Potter books are as popular there as they are in the UK.'

Publishing is an intricate and subjective business, but how was all this activity benefiting the author herself? Jo would have received a chunk of cash on signing that first contract from Bloomsbury, and the second instalment probably followed soon thereafter. So her financial situation was immediately improved, but it wasn't transformed.

It may sound mad in the light of what was to happen, but there was no guarantee at that time that *any* further payments would be forthcoming after the full advance had been paid. Bloomsbury was optimistic, and from the feedback Rosamund de la Hey was getting from readers of the manuscript, the signs were good, but even so, nobody would have been sufficiently confident to guarantee the author a certain level of income. Despite the magic of Harry Potter, there is still no crystal ball that gives accurate sales forecasts for publishers.

Jo would have had more money in her bank account than she'd had in years. But she wasn't letting herself relax. With the first book in her series sold, though not yet published, she was already hard at work on the second. Few writers at that stage in their careers would have been as adamant that there would be seven books. But Jo was. She had spent years meticulously planning the series, so she had a lot of writing to do.

There was no immediate guarantee that Bloomsbury would even buy the rights for the second book. Some publishers are cautious about commissioning a second book too quickly, nervous that the book that first attracted them was a flash in the pan. They may wait to see whether the first book sells well and how the author copes with the demands of promotion and publicity. Everybody knew of Jo's ambition for the series, but no publisher would have been prepared to plan that far ahead.

Of course, if a book does prove a bestseller, caution goes to the wind. The publisher will then be drumming their fingers on the table awaiting the second title. This is a double-edged sword and one of the reasons why so many authors find writing their second novel a far less enjoyable experience than the first. They are delighted that somebody wants their new book, but they now have the additional pressures of matching high expectations, and a deadline of the kind they have never known before.

All of a sudden there is a whole team of people including the editor, the marketing team, the designers, the publicists, the foreign rights team, the sales team and, of course, the readers, eagerly awaiting the arrival of that new manuscript.

Jo had found a great supporter in Barry and a new contract was forthcoming. But she was not by nature a risk taker and she had her daughter's care to consider. So she applied for a grant from the Scottish Arts Council. Their role was to give artists of all kinds the support they require to reach their full potential. The Council offered writers' bursaries which are effectively modest sums of money to enable authors to write their books. They are especially valued by unproven writers, who have shown promise but who may not yet have earned enough from their books to enable them to write full time. Writers like Jo Rowling in 1997.

Applications for these bursaries – which are still offered to writers – are made for all kinds of reasons. The author may need money to help them research a particular subject, or to visit a location that is significant to the book on which they are working. Or the application may come from a writer who simply needs money in order to buy time to write. In Jo's case the bursary enabled her to pay for childcare without having to find paid employment to cover the costs, so that she could continue writing.

The committee members considering the applications were so impressed by the chapters she submitted that in early 1997 they granted her £8,000 – a more generous bursary than she might have expected. (Later, the Scottish Arts Council would give a grant to the Scottish Braille Press to enable them to publish a Braille edition of the first novel.)

It was an indication of the confidence Jo's writing inspired in others. And the cheque meant that financially, Jo was reasonably secure. For a while.

Just before the official UK publication date of *Harry Potter and the Philosopher's Stone* on July 1st, 1997 the news broke that the auction for American rights had been won by Arthur A Levine, another inspiring and passionate editor of books for young people. For Jo, it was astonishing news: 'My agent called me at about 8pm one evening to tell me there was an auction going on in New York for the book. They were up to five figures. By the time he called me back at 10pm it was up to six figures. At 11pm my American editor, Arthur Levine, called me. The first words he said to me were "Don't panic". . . On one level I was obviously delighted but most of me froze.'

Panic isn't necessarily the first feeling we associate with such splendid news. But Arthur's comment was spookily accurate because Jo was overwhelmed by the news of the American sale. It caused her such anxiety that she found it difficult to write. She might have struggled to find the time and energy to get down to her manuscript, but she had never found it difficult to put pen to paper when the circumstances allowed. Arthur's perceptive advice marked the start of a strong bond between them. Perhaps more than anybody at that point, he realised that the future for Jo Rowling's books could be massive. He also realised that for his new author, the growing expectation might be intimidating.

In previous jobs, Arthur Levine had been involved in the acquisition of Brian Jacques' *Redwall* series and Philip Pullman's *His Dark Materials* trilogy so he had considerable experience and an excellent reputation. He is also an author in his own right. In the spring of that year he had been on the hunt for books to populate his new list – Arthur L Levine Books, an imprint within Scholastic Inc. He was given a set of proofs of *Harry Potter and the Philosopher's Stone* at the Bologna Book Fair and read them on the flight home.

In an interview with *The Washington Post* he said of that first reading, 'I remember loving the humour, thinking she is *so funny*, and thinking that here's a rare range of talents in a writer: somebody who can engage me emotionally and yet can make me laugh. And whose plot is *really* driving me forward.'

His enthusiasm for the story was immediate and he contacted the Christopher Little Literary Agency as soon as he could to enquire about the American rights. He would have been prepared to continue bidding had the auction not stopped where it did – at just over $100,000.

Arthur's offer marked a huge creative and financial breakthrough for Jo. It was now time to give up the day job.

CHAPTER SIX

Cracking America

ARTHUR Levine's confidence in his new author wasn't the no-brainer it now seems. Although America and Britain share the same language, their publishing industries are far from identical. British publishing for children has long held itself in high regard. Such classics as Kenneth Grahame's *The Wind in the Willows*, Lewis Carroll's *Alice's Adventures in Wonderland*, A A Milne's *Winnie the Pooh* and Beatrix Potter's beautifully observed little picture books had established British writers as amongst the best in the world. These writers had effectively created a new literature for young people, a market for which there had been very little fiction before the twentieth century.

Frank L Baum, Mark Twain, E B White and Louisa M Alcott were amongst the many influential American writers British children read. But on the whole, there hadn't been much appetite amongst British publishers for fiction from other countries. Now the balance was tipping. British children were developing a taste for books written in a different accent.

In the 1970s and 1980s, British television began to show many more American-made programmes. *Sesame Street* was a huge hit with preschool children in the UK, and there was also an influx of popular, often sentimental family-based comedy-dramas like *The Wonder Years* and *The Cosby Show*. The great British public has always lapped up Hollywood movies, but with traditional weekend family viewing slots increasingly occupied by American-made television shows, British children became even more familiar with American speech patterns, cadences and idioms.

It therefore made sense for British publishers to look to North America for fiction for young people. Judy Blume and Betsy Byars were proving hugely popular with British readers, especially girls, although their choice of subject matter didn't always meet with the approval of parents and teachers.

Judy Blume, especially, was pilloried for stories in which her characters grappled with the challenges of adolescence and the emotional upheavals and choices that accompanied it. Nowadays her novels appear quite tame, but books like *Are You There, God? It's Me*

Margaret?, *Blubber* and the particularly controversial *Forever* raised many an eyebrow when they were first published in the UK. Young readers fell on them, however, swapping and collecting complete sets, desperate to get their hands on each new title as it was published.

These novels were direct, contemporary, often reassuring and accessibly written, and the more they were frowned upon by adults, the more desirable they became. Irrepressible New Yorker Paula Danziger moved to London for much of the year to satisfy the UK demand for her to visit schools and appear at literary festivals. In such novels as *Divorce Express*, *It's an Aardvark-eat-Turtle World* and *The Cat Ate My Gymsuit* she combined straight-talking stories with an affectionate, quick-fire, funny delivery. She even presented a regular item about books on Saturday morning children's TV, a mighty accolade in the heady days of 1980s and 1990s.

Gradually, the appetite for American writers focused on books for young adults, with such authors as Cynthia Voigt, Paula Fox and Robert Cormier gathering a keen fan base. And gradually the critics and adult 'gate-keepers' – parents, librarians and teachers – began to realise that in most cases these were well-written books, the kind of novels that made readers think about life, the kind of novels they talked about with their friends.

So by the 1990s American publishers were not nearly

as reliant on British writing as they had once appeared. They were more than happy with home-grown talent. When Arthur Levine decided to buy the rights to *Harry Potter and the Philosopher's Stone* he was sticking his neck out by putting his faith in such a very British story. But even he must have had a slight wobble – he insisted that the title be changed to *Harry Potter and the Sorcerer's Stone*. He felt it would be easier for an American readership to understand than the original.

The sum paid by Arthur Levine for those American rights was unprecedented for a first book for children, and the news of the auction and its outcome attracted further press coverage in Britain on top of the articles and reviews that had already greeted Jo's début novel.

Inevitably, her own story was retold again and again, and the rags to riches element of her life before Blooms-bury's initial offer became an integral part of the whole Harry Potter press juggernaut which has since served the books so well, but has occasionally backfired on Jo herself.

CHAPTER SEVEN

Off the shelves

BACK in Britain in the summer of 1997, Rosamund de la Hey was hard at work publicising Harry Potter and his author. She and her colleagues at Bloomsbury believed they had a potential bestseller on their hands, but they were not complacent. Other publishers, some with greater publicity budgets, would be giving their own new books equally enthusiastic billing that summer. If she was confident that the press would give Jo Rowling, the author, coverage, she also needed to persuade the book trade to stock Rowling's book, preferably in large quantities, face out and in their window displays, and to talk it up.

Rosamund and her colleagues had organised a series of Bloomsbury roadshows that spring – regular regional events to which booksellers, journalists, librarians and people known as 'key influencers' are invited. At a roadshow the publisher presents the next season's books (for adults and children), before plying their guests with food and drink. They are good-natured, informal events and for booksellers in particular, a chance to talk to editors and writers they wouldn't normally meet. Jo attended Bloomsbury's Edinburgh roadshow. Her book was only briefly mentioned, although she was pointed out, standing at the back of the venue and she waved nervously at the assembled members of the book trade.

The extensive press coverage around the time of the publication of *Harry Potter and the Philosopher's Stone* in the UK was largely read by adults, of course. Children rarely look to newspapers to help them decide on their next book. But adults are the people who usually control a family's book budget, so the many articles and interviews about this new author were important. They made her stand out.

Booksellers were used to customers wandering round the children's department looking baffled and saying, 'I need something suitable for a 10 year-old. . .' In the summer of 1997 their customers were asking for this particular first novel by name. As a result, the sales of *Harry Potter and the Philosopher's Stone* were strong from the outset. Over the next few months Bloomsbury had to hit the reprint button again and again.

The initial hardback print-run – around 700 copies –

sold out almost immediately. Ordinarily that number would have been considered more than sufficient for a début novel. Hardbacks were declining in popularity at the time. All the research suggested they were too expensive and that young people preferred the informality of a portable, flexible paperback. If hardback editions were printed they were usually destined for libraries who were attracted by the robustness of the format compared with a paperback. Only the then top-selling authors like Anne Fine, Michael Morpurgo, Terry Pratchett and Jacqueline Wilson commanded sufficient loyalty to warrant a large print run of a comparatively pricey hardback.

But Jo Rowling – or J K Rowling as she was now officially known – was bucking the trend again. Bloomsbury Children's Books would be better prepared in future. The story about an orphan who discovered that he was a wizard after a miserable childhood being mistreated horribly by his aunt and uncle was capturing imaginations throughout Britain. The three-sided friendship between Harry, Hermione (often pronounced Hermy-One by those unfamiliar with the name) and Ron felt familiar to young readers, and to a certain extent the school setting with its teachers, dining rooms and subjects was familiar too. But there was far more to the books than that.

The vast invention of the world in which Harry finds

himself offers a rich mix of characters, settings, fun, fear, happiness and sadness and right from the start it was obvious to young readers that there was lots more from where that came. Jo's writing style was direct and unfussy, and her verbal and visual humour appealed enormously. The book was now out there – next the readers had the opportunity to meet its author.

The purpose of a book launch is, obviously, to celebrate the author's achievement in having reached this point in their career, to create a bit of a buzz around the new book, and also to sell copies. One of the perks of being at a book launch is to ask the author to sign your copy. Family and friends are expected to attend, along with interested booksellers and librarians and even other writers. A publisher hopes that at the end of the book launch guests will leave sufficiently impressed by it all to become enthusiastic ambassadors for the new book.

Rosamund de la Hey and Andrew Jaffrey-Smith, the Bloomsbury sales rep at that time in Scotland, arranged a launch event for *Harry Potter and the Philosopher's Stone* in John Smith and Co, a traditional independent Glasgow bookseller. Grainne Cooney, then the manager of John Smith's children's department had requested the event – she was keen to invite a class of local school children.

'I remember getting a set of proofs from Bloomsbury,' she said. 'It [*Harry Potter and the Philosopher's Stone*] was such a breath of fresh air. There was nothing like it around at the time and it just blew me away. I had gone along to the Bloomsbury Road Show in Glasgow and I remember Jo standing up to talk about her book. . . She was so nervous but I sat there with a huge grin because I loved the book and was enjoying hearing her talk about it. Afterwards she said she was really glad I was there as I was the only kids' buyer who had read it so no-one had a clue what she was talking about – *a boy wizard*, for goodness sake?!'

The gathering to celebrate the launch of Jo's first novel took place in the basement of the shop. Grainne remembers it well. 'I made a big effort. I got somebody to blow up the illustration of the train on the front cover of the book, and a friend from BBC Scotland got me a sound effect of a steam train whistle to open proceedings. Having not done many events in the shop I was very nervous – as it turned out, Jo was a lot more nervous than me. I remember her having a sneaky fag in the loo before going on to talk to the school kids.'

Jo read the passage in which Harry is allocated his first wand. She was shy and seemed slightly awkward, but she was obviously delighted to talk quietly with the children who attended. Suddenly her world was also theirs. It was the beginning of a bond that has characterised her career. Jo looked relieved to see the book finally in other people's hands and she signed copies until they ran out.

Later that summer, Jo Rowling had accepted an invitation to take part in the Edinburgh International Book Festival which takes place every August under canvas in Charlotte Square Gardens, the grassy square which marks the western boundary of the city's elegant George Street. The Festival was well established, but audiences in Edinburgh can be conservative and they don't tend to take a punt on a new author. That year the Festival had added a Native American-style tepee to the range of tents available for events. It had room for about twenty people, at the most, and the seating was on straw bales and colourful rugs which had been flung on top of matting. It was cosy and informal but damp weather and a lavish sprinkling of lavender oil combined to create a strangely sweet farmyard aroma.

Kathryn Ross, then working for Scottish Book Trust, was one of a number of people introducing children's events that year at the book festival. 'I'd read the manuscript, seen Jo at the Edinburgh Roadshow and heard her read in Glasgow, so I was already well and truly "hooked on Harry". Despite her nerves beforehand, it was a relaxed and happy event, with the audience consisting mainly of family and friends of the author and festival staff. It seems incredible now, and with the benefit of hindsight, to think that J K Rowling's first book festival audience was a little group of children and adults sitting on scratchy straw bales and slightly damp rugs in a tepee. There might have been a bit of squirming to get comfortable at first but we were soon enthralled by the magic of the story and by Jo herself.'

Across the UK Jo's book continued to sell well. She put down a deposit on her first home, finally bidding farewell to the world of benefits and dependency she had so loathed. But she has never forgotten what that period of her life felt like, and in the future, when she had the chance, she would take every opportunity to use those memories to present the world with some uncomfortable truths.

CHAPTER EIGHT

Creating shelf space

IN the early days following publication most of the newspaper coverage concentrated more on Jo Rowling's life story than on reviews of her book. Bloomsbury had suggested that she use initials – Jo borrowed the K from her grandmother, Kathleen – instead of her full name because they didn't want the fact that the book had been written by a woman to put boys off buying *Harry Potter and the Philosopher's Stone*.

As so many of the articles and interviews were accompanied by photographs of the attractive young writer, her cover was blown right from the start. Boys seem to have coped well with the sex of the author.

Anne Johnstone printed her review of the book in *The Herald* on August 16th, 1997. 'A brilliant début from Edinburgh teacher, Joanne Rowling. An utterly absorbing fantasy novel which takes off on the first page. Well-drawn characters and a marvellously imaginative fast-paced story about an orphan who is forced to live with his beastly suburban relatives – that is, until he discovers that he is a wizard.'

The supplement had a 'back to school' emphasis and Jo's was one of five short reviews for books Anne Johnstone recommended for 8- to 12-year-olds. The others were for Jacqueline Wilson's *The Lottie Project*, Philip Pullman's *Northern Lights*, *The Sleepover Club at Frankie's* by Rose Impey and *Water Wings* by the Australian writer Morris Gleitzman. Jo was in excellent company, company that should have given any newly published author encouragement.

Both Jacqueline Wilson and Philip Pullman were then – and remain – popular and extremely well reviewed. But despite writing many splendid novels they hadn't always enjoyed such success or recognition. In an inspired decision, Transworld had invited Nick Sharratt to create a distinctive look for Jacqueline's novels, transforming her career. His deceptively subtle line drawings, almost but not quite cartoons, proved perfect for her particular style of storytelling and the duo continue to enjoy huge success.

Philip Pullman's *Northern Lights* had been published to great and immediate acclaim on both sides of the Atlantic Ocean but, like Jacqueline, that level of recognition had been relatively slow in coming. Philip Pullman's *His Dark Materials* trilogy catapulted their author into a life transformed by fame, significant fortune and, in time, a major Hollywood film deal. He has also become something of a pundit, often sought by the media to comment on aspects of the world of books and literacy.

Rose Impey's *Sleepover Club* series enjoyed international sales and led to an engaging Australian television series. For the Leicestershire-based author the experience was exciting and life-changing but she was no one-trick pony and Rose Impey continues to make her living writing much-loved books for children of all ages.

Two Weeks with the Queen, Morris Gleitzman's breakthrough novel in the UK had caught the eye of Marion Lloyd, an editor with Pan, and when she bought the rights for publication in Britain in 1989 readers fell for what Australian children had enjoyed for some time – Gleitzman's laid-back, humorous storytelling with its signature emotional punch. *Water Wings* was classic Morris Gleitzman – the hilarious, heart-warming adventure of Pearl and her adored guinea pig, Winston.

The newly published J K Rowling might have been encouraged and inspired by the careers of her four fellow authors. Book sales were going well, but she wasn't to know that before long she would find herself on the same prize short-lists, and that she and Philip Pullman would share the dubious honour of having their books banned in some parts of America.

In the same day's paper, there was an interview with the incomparable Shirley Hughes. She is the author and illustrator of the much loved *Dogger* and *Alfie Gets in First*, amongst many other award-winning picture books. That summer she had celebrated her 70th birthday and the publication of a new Alfie story, *Alfie and the Birthday Surprise*. Shirley Hughes' long career has been steady and successful. An enormously likeable lady, she still seems to love the world she observes through the characters in her stories. In that article she explained: 'The bedrock of three to five-year-olds is the utterly perennial archaic things that they do, like laying two conkers on a leaf and saying "this is my shop".'

Jo Rowling, the mother of a small girl, might have smiled at that. And J K Rowling might, or might not have taken note of another comment Shirley Hughes made, when it was pointed out that this was the first book about Alfie in five years. 'I need to refresh myself,' she explained. 'I'd hate to be on a treadmill with Alfie. I'd lose my enthusiasm for him.'

Losing enthusiasm for writing was not something that worried Jo Rowling, although there were times when the words flowed more easily than others. Losing enthusiasm for the world in which she suddenly found herself up to her armpits was a problem.

In those early interviews she had given away a lot about her life. She wasn't the first person to have left a broken marriage, and she wasn't the only single parent to have found it difficult to cope. She wasn't the first person to have lost a mother far too young either. But all that information was now in the public domain, and when combined with her obvious commercial success, Jo's easy relationship with some members of the press became strained.

Some found themselves frozen out, as if she felt she had said too much. She is a chatty, entertaining, sometimes indiscreet conversationalist, so to an extent, they knew a great deal about her. Most journalists understood what was on and off record. The less scrupulous amongst them didn't and wanted to know more. Jo was shocked: 'It never occurred to me in a million years that people would search my dustbins, put a long-lens camera on me on the beach or bang on the door of one of my oldest friends and offer her money to talk about me.'

There are inevitably downsides to success and the celebrity that goes with it and although Jo found some of the attention distressing, it was the attention to her family, and particularly her daughter, that she would find totally unacceptable.

CHAPTER NINE
Hollywood calls

IN the autumn of 1997 *Harry Potter and the Philosopher's Stone* won the prestigious Nestlé Smarties Book Award, a prize in which the final decisions were made by young people. Early the following year Jo walked away with the award for Children's Book of the Year at the British Book Awards – which was a clear indication that the book trade was in love with her – and she went on to win the Federation of Children's Book Groups' Children's Book Award in the summer of 1998, another award in which children make the selections.

In a relatively short space of time those young readers had become familiar with the characters of Harry, Hermione and Ron, and with words like 'muggle', 'knuts' and 'quidditch'. *Harry Potter and the Philosopher's Stone* had ended with Harry delighting in the prospect of making his cousin Dudley Dursley's life a misery during the summer holiday. Readers couldn't wait to find out exactly what that had entailed and what would happen next at Hogwarts School of Witchcraft and Wizardry.

Arthur Levine, watching from his Broadway office in New York, must have been rubbing his hands with glee as he and his colleagues planned the American launch of *Harry Potter and the Sorcerer's Stone* in October 1998. A ten-city tour had been planned to ensure that by the end J K Rowling's first novel, and J K Rowling herself would be as well-known and popular there as it was in Britain.

It wasn't long after the publication of *Harry Potter and the Philosopher's Stone* that various film companies began to court Jo, intent on buying the rights to make films of her books. At first she turned them all down. Her concern wasn't the money. It was largely that by signing away the rights to the books, she could lose control over them, and over the characters she had so painstakingly nurtured over the years. Yes, the seven books were all carefully plotted and planned, but at this point she hadn't even signed off the final draft of the second novel. She didn't want her plans to be compromised by the demands of a powerful Hollywood film company.

There aren't many writers with the courage to turn

down Hollywood so early in their careers. But it must have been clear to Jo and to her literary agent that as the excitement surrounding the books grew, her refusal to sell the film rights wouldn't stop the film industry trying to buy them. Jo remained directly involved in the discussions and for somebody who had no experience of the film industry at that time, it must have been a steep learning curve.

With her first book out, the second finally completed, and the third underway, she was also grappling with her new life as a published author, and the pressure on her must have been intense. But she held her nerve. Everybody knows that a film for young people is far more than simply the film itself – at the very least there would be merchandising, toys, DVDs, games. . . And then there would be issues about copyright, casting, and script approval.

Many writers simply take the view that they aren't sufficiently powerful to influence a film studio's decision-making process. They accept the best offer, then leave the stage to the directors, producers and script-writers. But Jo Rowling was not prepared to take a back seat. From the outset she refused to hand over control. She felt she couldn't. And for one very good reason. J K Rowling was the only person in the world who knew how Harry Potter's story ended. There was never any question of changing her mind about that. After all, she had already written the final chapter.

Of course, her literary agent and his colleagues would have been familiar with this kind of negotiation on behalf of other authors but even they must have been surprised by the speed at which things were developing. Film offers and talk of merchandise and games would certainly have been a cause for celebration in Christopher Little's office, but it was important to keep everybody's feet on the ground, to secure the best possible outcome for the author, and for her books. Although the responsibility for any final decision would be Jo's, her agent would have been concerned to give her best advice. But he can't have been unimpressed by her diligence and tenacity.

With all this going on, it is not surprising that in the summer of 1997 *Harry Potter and the Chamber of Secrets* proved quite a challenge for Jo to complete. She met the deadline she had agreed with Bloomsbury, but then asked for the manuscript back and was allowed a further six weeks to ensure that she was happy with it. Barry Cunningham had left the company, and she was now being edited by Emma Matthewson at Bloomsbury Children's Books. Any writer values a good relationship with their editor and when editors leave it can take a while to settle into a good working relationship.

Emma is a very different personality to Barry, but in many ways she was now the perfect editor for Jo: loyal, discreet, bright and committed. In an interview in 2000, Jo revealed that the change may even have had its advantages. 'In *Philosopher's Stone* I had a game of chess between Harry and Ron which Ron won by using a particularly violent bishop. My editor made me take it out. He didn't want me to have a bad bishop. Well, he's back. I have a different editor now.'

Harry Potter and the Chamber of Secrets was published in Britain in July 1998. Readers flocked to the bookshops in such numbers that the second of Jo's novels shot straight to the number one slot in the best-seller lists, outselling adult bestsellers. That in itself made the news. Children's books simply didn't do that kind of thing. The success of Jo's first book was definitely not a one-off. Harry Potter was here to stay.

CHAPTER TEN

Publication dates

WOULD J K Rowling keep up the momentum?

Inevitably when something out of the ordinary happens in a particular retail market there are those who are sceptical, and the world of children's books is no exception. Jo had set herself a cracking pace. The first four novels ended up being published a year apart in Britain, with each book longer than its predecessor.

Many of her American readers, frustrated by the scheduled June 1999 publication date on that side of the Atlantic, bought *Harry Potter and the Chamber of Secrets* direct from British online booksellers. These were readers Arthur Levine wanted for his edition so he speeded up his publishing schedule, timing *Harry Potter and the Prisoner of Azkaban* for publication in October 1999, three months after the launch of the British edition. Thereafter, the American editions and the British editions would be published on the same day.

The first two British launches had been given publication dates on which the public could expect to find the books on bookshop shelves. Every new book is allocated a publication date, but it was – and is – rare for them to be enforced. Few booksellers were particularly careful about adhering to them but it was rarely an issue. Most books are despatched by publishers' warehouses so that they arrive at the bookshops close to publication day anyway.

But in the case of *Harry Potter and the Prisoner of Azkaban*, Bloomsbury decided to sharpen things up, and to make a feature of the publication date. It would ensure publicity for the book within the book trade, giving booksellers an opportunity to make the most of the event, and it might attract some press attention too.

Bloomsbury must have been confident of strong sales, but once again, they were not complacent. This was, after all, the third book in the series. The media might be wearying of the annual 'Here's yet another book about wizards by that once destitute single mother who made a cup of coffee last for three hours in an Edinburgh café' story they tended to churn out. Bloomsbury needed to find another angle.

Jo's wariness of the press created a further challenge. She had given interview after interview over the previous two years and she didn't believe that a similar level of exposure was critical for the new book's success.

In 1997 Jo had finally settled on Warner Bros. as the film company she trusted sufficiently to take Harry and his friends to the big screen. They had agreed to her having script approval – a huge concession for a film studio. Her determination and stubbornness had paid off. Despite initial reservations about her insistence that the films should be made in Britain with British actors, and that there could be no films made about Harry Potter other than those based on her seven books, Warner Bros. clearly recognised that the compromises were worth it. This was a property with huge potential and they bought rights options on the first two books for a considerable sum.

The massive enthusiasm for the books persuaded them that they would shoot themselves in the foot were they to veer too far away from J K Rowling's storylines. Reader loyalty towards the author has been a key feature of Jo's career. Disappoint her and they could disappoint her readers. They needed to keep them on-side if the films were to be successful.

For Bloomsbury and all Jo's growing team of publishers throughout the world, a film deal was excellent news. Films and television series can result in excellent book sales. But the film of *Harry Potter and the Philosopher's Stone* wouldn't be released until 2001, which gave everybody plenty of time to keep reading. It was important to keep the world's attention firmly focussed on the books.

That world now included adults. It is said that it was the sight of embarrassed adults on the London Underground reading *Harry Potter and the Philosopher's Stone* behind their newspapers that led Bloomsbury to issue exactly the same book in 1998 with a different cover designed for grown-ups. This marketing decision added to the series' commercial success. Harry Potter was of course well known, but now the books were reaching cult status amongst adults who didn't necessarily come to them through reading the books aloud to eager offspring.

But for the launch of the third novel Bloomsbury focussed on the original young readers. They were the people who had whipped up previously unheard-of sales figures for books one and two, and they would be rewarded with some Harry Potter fun.

The key to success was in providing a focal point in the day, so Rosamund de la Hey and her colleagues at Bloomsbury decided that there would be an official and sacrosanct 'launch moment' – 3.45pm – within the publication day of Thursday July 8th, 1999. In a pre-publication interview with *The Independent* that June,

Rosamund said, 'It's been prompted by the booksellers who were phoning me in January saying, "When's the next one coming out?" That got us thinking about the timing. . . Hopefully there'll be queues of kids up and down the streets waiting for their copies. It's very much a visual exercise.'

In press briefings somebody cleverly suggested that because the book would be unavailable until that specific moment, Harry Potter devotees wouldn't be tempted to truant from school in order to get hold of their copy. Would they have truanted? We'll never know, because bookshops welcomed the idea of the after-school launch. It provided them with a handy focal point at which to make a bit of a splash.

A Birmingham bookshop displayed a copy of *Harry Potter and the Prisoner of Azkaban* in a cage with a security guard standing by, liberating it on the dot of 3.45pm. Many others hired magicians and organised competitions, encouraging children to come dressed as their favourite character. The release of the first film was still two years away at this point. Nobody knew then that Harry Potter looked like Daniel Radcliffe, then filming his début role as the young David Copperfield for a BBC dramatisation of the Charles Dickens novel.

The focus on the 3.45pm publication moment distracted from the fact that Jo Rowling would not make any official appearances. In an interview the following month she explained, 'I wasn't hiding. I just needed to work.' She was grateful to Bloomsbury for having let her off any official launch appearances, but she was aware that her American publisher was anxious for a reappearance on that side of the Atlantic. 'The books are going well but sales could be increased by a lot more promotion,' she said.

Although she was not visible for the launch of the British edition, she had agreed to a three week tour of North America later that autumn, and Scholastic Inc. was preparing for it by hiring bodyguards to impose crowd control.

CHAPTER ELEVEN

Let the madness commence

JO'S sell-out event at the 1999 Edinburgh International Book Festival in August – she had moved to
the biggest of the tents with seating for over 400 –
followed a straightforward format with which she was
comfortable. She would read an extract from the new book
at the beginning and then open the floor to questions.

Some authors struggle to get their audience to ask
questions at that kind of event. The unfamiliar surroundings and shyness in front of a crowd of people they don't
know can be inhibiting. But that has never been true of
an event with J K Rowling. Her teaching experience meant
that she now ran her Q&A sessions with easy confidence,
and she clearly revelled in the grilling her readers gave
her, congratulating them on their clever questions,
carefully considering how much information she could
give away without compromising the future books,

teasing them with hints about what might – or might not – happen next. Threats of future deaths were especially tantalising.

Her informal approach, combined with a dry sense of humour, delight in her audience's often nerdy knowledge of her books, self-deprecation and the occasional raucous laugh created a relaxed atmosphere. The children treated her like one of them and she responded warmly.

But outside the tent, life was more challenging. The price of fame was taking its toll and arrangements were made to take the pressure off. Jo's signings were carefully orchestrated – no photos, no dedications, only one book per child. Her publicists became adept at time-saving strategies, deftly opening the book for her at the title page, pushing it along for her to sign quickly and hand to the next child in the queue. Chat was not encouraged, but sometimes Jo couldn't help herself and a comment from a child would lead to a brief conversation until the minders moved things along again, re-establishing the flip-shove-sign-handover rhythm.

Most authors have to spend some time in the public eye these days, but Jo was increasingly uncomfortable about giving up so much time to touring and events. She wanted to be home with her daughter, and writing.

'In all of this madness I'm still trying to bring up my child, mostly by myself,' she said in an interview in 2000.

'At the moment priority No. 1 is Jessica, priority No. 2 is the quality of the books and there are lots of things jockeying for third place.' This wasn't the voice of somebody who was enjoying life very much. As she became less and less 'available' there were inevitable grumbles from the press and resentment from some authors who felt their festival events were overshadowed by her rare appearances – or non-appearances.

At an award ceremony in Edinburgh in 2006 her editor travelled from London to accept the prize on Jo's behalf. There were a few raised eyebrows when she explained to those present that Jo couldn't attend because she was too busy writing. Jo's fellow shortlisted authors were particularly unimpressed. *They* had found the time.

Professional jealousy was inevitable, and decisions like the one not to attend that local event didn't help. But it was indicative of J K Rowling's transition from bestselling author to celebrity author. Outside her own launch events and television interviews, she began to limit her public appearances to major industry and charitable gatherings. If she kept the media happy by posing on red carpets from time to time, her private life might be left relatively undisturbed. She was learning to manipulate the press before it manipulated her.

It is almost unknown for a children's event at a book festival to attract any media attention – but J K Rowling was the exception. Even if she addressed not a single word to the press there was no letting up. Her ex-husband sold his story to a tabloid newspaper in the autumn of 1999. It was a terrible blow. The coverage wasn't only about her, or her writing, it was about her daughter too, and she found this new level of intrusion and exposure deeply distressing.

The Christopher Little Literary Agency became more visibly protective of their client. There could be nothing casual or spontaneous about her professional life from now on. All her publishers' activities and plans were even more closely scrutinised. No detail was left unconfirmed. It was not a comfortable time.

But elsewhere, the books maintained their extraord-inary momentum.

Alyx Price, now Consumer, Marketing and Commun-ications Director, Scholastic UK, was a bookseller with Waterstone's in the late 1990s. She was responsible for compiling the second edition of the *Waterstone's Guide to Children's Books* – a useful publication for book buyers – and remembers a meeting with Rosamund de la Hey in which Rosamund pressed a newly delivered finished early copy of *Harry Potter and the Chamber of Secrets* into her hands, keen for her to include it in the Guide.

'But it was the third book that really took off. Even

though she stopped doing the industry circuit – appearing at festivals and schools – the sales kept going and going. That was when I became aware of the book dealers' interest. In my branch [of Waterstone's] we didn't get any first editions of *Harry Potter and the Prisoner of Azkaban* and that mattered a great deal to people. And the whole Harry Potter thing changed the way publishers published their lead titles. I remember when I was working at Macmillan Children's Books in 2002 we published *Molly Moon's Incredible Book of Hypnotism* by Georgia Byng and much thought went into this whole idea of a first edition and the added value it created. It was a useful hook to send a first edition out to influencers in the children's book world.'

Bloomsbury had taken on board the growing enthusiasm for first editions of J K Rowling's books. Grainne Cooney, the organiser of that first launch event in Glasgow in 1997, was an early beneficiary. 'I remember I asked Jo to sign a copy of the book but there were so few hardbacks there that she said she would sign one and get Andrew Jaffrey-Smith, the Bloomsbury rep, to send it to me. He was as good as his word and later that book was sold at auction. The proceeds helped me put in an offer for my little cottage up here in the Scottish Highlands. So I'm not ashamed to say that Harry Potter was life-changing for me. In fact I think it weaved a bit of magic for me!'

The adult editions had proved remarkably popular, so in September 1999, Bloomsbury published the first of the clothbound special editions and with its striking red livery embossed with J K Rowling's signature, the new edition of *Harry Potter and the Philosopher's Stone* created another set of books for collectors of all ages. Bloomsbury's commitment to beautifully produced books had found a worthy and lucrative focus on their children's list, and Harry Potter fans snapped them up.

Every other publisher was looking for ways to reclaim some of the ground they had lost to Bloomsbury and the Harry Potter novels. They wanted the attention and they wanted the sales too. But creating a bestseller isn't easy. For a start, you have to find the writers to write them and that takes time. Then you have to get your marketing and publicity right. The goalposts kept changing and publishers looked around for other writers who might generate the same enjoyment and loyalty, the same buzz. Harry Potter cast a long shadow, but that wasn't necess-arily a bad thing.

'The press had made a big deal of Atemis Fowl being the new Harry Potter,' says Alyx Price, 'and then the story that Georgia Byng was the new J K Rowling. . . it was amazing how often that story could be repeated for other characters and authors.'

Scholastic UK was fortunate in already having Philip

Pullman's *His Dark Materials* trilogy on their list. These books were demanding, literary novels and his readers anticipated each new title with huge excitement. All of them won significant children's book awards, but *The Amber Spyglass* was notable for winning the Whitbread Book of the Year in 2002, the first time a book published for young people had ever done so. Adults were fans too, of course. His events at book festivals were popular with readers of all ages, many of whom looked far too young to be able to read the books, let alone understand them. The evident appeal of Pullman's books gave children's publishers the courage to be more adventurous in their acquisitions.

A feature of the novels by both Philip Pullman and J K Rowling was that children would read and re-read them, mining them for details that might shed light on what was to come. Their close interrogation of the texts was impressive, if obsessive, as anybody familiar with the on-line communities will know. Discussion and debate was part and parcel of the reading process for huge numbers of readers. J K Rowling's three central characters and their classmates were growing up – a narrative strategy that some regarded as foolhardy. But of course those first readers grew up alongside them, their own emotional compass developing alongside those of Harry, Hermione and Ron. It worked like a dream.

But there were interesting consequences. Having won

the Nestlé Smarties Book Prize for her first three novels, Jo decided that the fourth should not be submitted, feeling that *Harry Potter and the Prisoner of Azkaban* was now too old for the 9 to 11 age category. Some of her competitors must have breathed a sigh of relief. Others felt patronised, that her decision devalued the prize. But there was no let up. Awards kept rolling in from all over the world.

The decision drastically to reduce the number of J K Rowling's live events caused considerable unrest amongst organisers for whom she had become an important draw, but Alyx Price believes that it made space for other authors. 'She let other authors succeed, you might argue, by stepping back.'

Many will find that a hard theory to swallow. The impact of the Harry Potter books' success inevitably skewed the market, accounting for a huge proportion of sales of children's books. Some authors found the innocent questions directed at them by their own audiences – Do you know J K Rowling? Are you as rich as J K Rowling? – dispiriting and even insulting. But their publishers were not standing by with their chins on the ground. They couldn't afford to be. Author visibility was the most effective way for them to claw back sales.

Anthony Horowitz's *Groosham Grange*, a comedy fantasy adventure about a boy with magical powers published in 1998, had been successful, but not hugely so. Instead of trying to jump on the Harry Potter band-wagon, Walker Books saw in their author's writing the potential for something different but equally character-driven and inventive, so *Stormbreaker,* the first novel about Alex Rider, the James Bond-type orphaned teenager was published in 2000. The novel was an immediate success and launched a series which has gone on to sell in millions the world over. Anthony's events are routinely sold out.

Jacqueline Wilson and Terry Pratchett were the main fiction stars for Random House in the late 1990s, but they knew better than to put all their eggs in one basket. Amongst several new acquisitions they trumpeted the arrival of *Pure Dead Magic* by Debi Gliori, the first of the Strega Borgia Chronicles, published in 2001 with an eye-catching and tactile velvet-effect cover, and *The Amulet of Samarkand* by Jonathan Stroud, the first in the outstanding Bartimaeus trilogy.

In fact any book competes with any other book but the Harry Potter series had created a whole new economic landscape. Author advances increased as publishers competed to snap up the next big talent, terrified of losing out again. To recoup the advances, publishers spent previously unheard-of amounts to ensure a high profile in bookshops and the supermarket chains, which were increasingly interested in profiting from this apparently lucrative area of the market. But despite undeniable successes, it was hard to envisage any book toppling the Harry Potter titles from their record-breaking perch.

The dominance of the Harry Potter books created a fascinating crisis in America. At *The New York Times* in 2000 there was growing debate over the future of their influential bestseller lists. J K Rowling's first novel had edged into the hardback bestseller list, but with the success of books two and three, the top three slots in the hardback lists had been occupied for well over a year by Harry Potter titles. And with the fourth book on the way there was concern that other deserving books (for adults) were being kept out.

The debate says much about the general attitude towards books for children. If the spaces had been occupied for so long by particular adult novels, there would have been no alternative except to grin and bear it. Eventually it was decided that a separate list should be created for children's books, liberating spaces for adult titles. This was a decision with which many disagreed, throwing up all kinds of issues about readership and what constitutes a book for children. Further controversy was added in 2004, when yet another list was created for series of children's books – and the Harry Potter books were shifted once again.

Some writers were glad of *The New York Times'*

decision, believing that it gave more children's books more exposure. Others felt that it diminished the genre. It remains a contentious issue but the fact remained that children's books were selling well. Alan Gibbons, Eleanor Updale, Georgia Byng, David Almond, Garth Nix, Michael Morpurgo, Neil Gaiman, Christopher Paolini and Meg Cabot were amongst the other authors doing well during this buoyant period for children's books.

Children's booksellers too enjoyed the increased profile of a job which was often seen as a stepping stone to better things in the adult book department. Specialist children's booksellers had been amongst the first to 'hand sell' *Harry Potter and the Philosopher's Stone.* Customers now turned to them with confidence and trust.

But with the changes came a change in expectations, and that wasn't necessarily such a good thing. Historically new children's books rarely made a splash. New titles were expected to cultivate a readership over time and to grow in popularity. Those with staying power were the books that would still be in print years later. The changes meant that now books were expected to prove themselves within a much shorter space of time. They weren't given long. Those that didn't sell well and quickly were shipped back to the publisher with indecent haste, giving potential readers no time to find them, either on the shelves of their bookshop or through word of mouth.

It's a particular problem for new writers, very few of whom get the kind of extensive media coverage that J K Rowling attracted. There are those who believe that in the current climate a writer like Roald Dahl, who increased his readership gradually over a number of years, would not have been given the luxury of enough time to become popular.

But for now the mood was generally upbeat and positive. In 1999 Quentin Blake was appointed the first ever Children's Laureate, a role that had been devised by the writer Michael Morpurgo and his great friend, the poet Ted Hughes. The post was timely, benefiting from the increased media attention being paid to children's books and highlighting the range of talent amongst writers and illustrators for children in Britain. Quentin Blake was the ideal inaugural Children's Laureate. First published in 1961, he was much loved by children and adults as the illustrator of most of Roald Dahl's children's stories, and as the creator of such classic picture books as *Mr Magnolia* and *Cockatoos*.

Most publishers tended to stay clear of a Harry Potter publication date, deciding that it would be impossible to compete with the increasing hype and hoopla. But the publisher Faber and Faber took a deep breath and faced the challenge head on. They decided to make use of the launch of *Harry Potter and the Order of the Phoenix* in 2003 to help catapult their new find – a former vicar, G P Taylor – into the bestseller list with his début novel, *Shadowmancer*.

'*The biggest new thing in young adult fiction since Harry Potter. . .*' and '. . . *the biggest event in children's fiction since Harry Potter*' trumpeted the quotes on the proof copies they sent out ahead of the June publication date. It worked. *Shadowmancer* sold well, though perhaps not in Harry Potter quantities.

Other publishers looked to their backlist – books that they had published some time before but which weren't getting the deserved attention – in the hope that they might benefit from reflected glory and pick up sales. Susan Cooper, Ursula le Guin, Diana Wynne Jones and Eva Ibbotson were all outstanding writers who might have wondered why their careers hadn't taken off with quite the same energy as J K Rowling's. All four had sold impressive numbers of books over the years and established a devoted readership, but it was Eva Ibbotson who could have been particularly miffed. In *The Secret of Platform 13*, published in 1994, a forgotten door on a railway platform opens to reveal a magical kingdom. Ibbotson's response to the inevitable loaded comments was characteristically positive, telling Amanda Craig in *The Times* that she 'would like to shake (J K Rowling) by the hand. I think we all borrow from others as writers.'

CHAPTER TWELVE

A different set of rules

*H*ARRY *Potter and the Goblet of Fire*, J K Rowling's fourth novel, was scheduled for release in English-speaking countries on July 8th, 2000. After the success of the publication 'moment' for *Harry Potter and the Prisoner of Azkaban*, Bloomsbury began the countdown to the new book's arrival. But in setting the publication date for what was arguably the most anticipated book ever, nobody – the author, the editor, the printers, the publicity team, the designers or anybody else involved in a book's production – had any room for manoeuvre.

The main pressure though was on the author and that novel seems to have given her a particularly bumpy ride. Jo discovered a hole in the plot which led to a consider-able rethink, and she has admitted that the ninth chapter had to be rewritten thirteen times. It doesn't take much of an imagination to understand how Jo Rowling felt as she struggled to weld her narrative together again in order to meet the deadlines on which so much depended. The pressure would have been immense at the best of times, but these were not the best of times.

Both her editors admitted that the manuscript for the fourth novel had been delivered later than anticipated. In an interview with *The New York Observer* in July 2000 her Bloomsbury editor, Emma Matthewson, said diplomatically, 'The manuscript was delivered at the end of February which should not be taken as a normal schedule for publishing.'

Arthur Levine told the same newspaper that the delivery date had been some time around mid-April. 'It's a pivotal book,' he said. 'Her concern was to ensure she crafted her story in just the right way.'

Whatever the tension behind the scenes, both editors had faith in their author. 'I was always in constant communication with Jo,' said Emma, 'and she would tell me how she was getting on. . . I have complete trust in her.'

Jo herself later admitted to the pressure they were all under in an answer she gave a fan about a continuity issue in the book. Admitting there was a minor glitch she said, 'We were all very sleep-deprived at the time.'

The book was listed in Scholastic's catalogue under the title *Harry Potter and the Doomspell Tournament*, but in mid-May that title was dropped. In an online chat that May, Jo referred to it as a working title. Both Bloomsbury and Arthur L Levine Books would not reveal the new title, referring to it now as *Harry Potter Four*.

If this reflected any conflict, the ever-ingenious publicity team made a virtue of it, announcing that the author wanted the title to remain secret until publication day. For the first time, no proofs were made available, and no advance copies issued. Reviewers were told that they, like all readers, would have to wait until publication day. Anybody working with the book in any context was asked to sign a confidentiality agreement.

By this time, Harry Potter fans had a growing presence on the internet. In fact online marketing was being done for the books very effectively by the fans. There were – and are – websites full of all kinds of information about the books, the author, and the publishing programme. Any dribble of new information was posted immediately, and the incessant online chatter batted back and forth from terminal to terminal around the globe created a growing virtual background noise as the publication date loomed. If the author was insisting on keeping the title secret, that didn't stop her fans trying to work it out. In fact the title was leaked to the *Daily Telegraph* on June 25th and confirmed a few days later. The ploy hadn't worked perfectly, but it had definitely helped *Harry Potter and the Goblet of Fire* to remain centre stage. And at midnight on July 8th, there it was, weighing in at a hefty 636 pages.

Jo was not allowed to launch this book in her absence. A four-day tour on a train, renamed The Hogwarts Express was organised by Rosamund de la Hey and her colleagues at Bloomsbury, setting off from platform nine-and-three-quarters at King's Cross Station in London, of course. There were ecstatic crowds at all eight stops as the specially liveried steam train wended its way north, ending the journey in Perth.

Stephen Fry, who has provided the voice of the books on the British audio editions, interviewed Jo Rowling on board and she reiterated a comment she had made before. 'I often think I was temperamentally best suited to being a moderately successful author. I didn't have the faintest idea what I was walking into. But then nor did anyone else. . .' Given the scale of the celebrations and the level of excitement generated by the wait for the book, and then its arrival, and her rousing send off from each station, the remark is telling.

The train journey was a great success by all accounts and Jo enjoyed herself. But she must have been aware that when she disembarked at Perth station life wasn't going to get any simpler.

By that stage she was deep in discussions about the

film of *Harry Potter and the Philosopher's Stone* which would be released the following year. Her determination that the cast would be a British one must have required constant monitoring and she was regularly consulted by the director, Chris Columbus, needing details for sets and other information which only Jo could provide. She was also inundated with merchandising proposals. The merchandising had always made her uneasy but she recognised its inevitability, and responded character-istically by insisting on close personal involvement with what was being developed in the name of her books.

The scale of her creative and financial success brought with it business responsibilities. Jo had employed staff to help her manage the increasing number of fan letters she received. She has always credited her sister and her friends with giving her support when she needed it but her personal and professional world now necessitated a more formal structure.

Jo's Personal Assistant, Fiddy Henderson was the perfect appointment – Jo has described her as 'indefatig-able, invaluable, indispensable' – providing a warm and polite buffer to those – including me – who made proposals that Jo couldn't possibly accept. (Scottish Book Trust now needed J K Rowling rather more than she had ever needed us.)

'I never was in a position where I signed a piece of

paper saying that this would happen,' she explained to Stephen Fry during that interview onboard The Hogwarts Express. But there was no going back.

Later that year she stepped onto a podium in the Toronto Skydome and read – once they'd finished screaming – to over 16,000 children. She has likened the experience to that of being one of the four Beatles. But there was only one J K Rowling. She needed to find a way to bring what she referred to as 'the madness' under control, and to enjoy the fruits of her success. Along with Fiddy Henderson, Jo settled into a working relationship with Colman Getty, a respected public relations agency with experience of the book trade and, at the time, an office in Edinburgh. Their help in co-ordinating Jo's public appearances and managing the incessant demands from the press would prove invaluable in all aspects of her professional life.

Jo Rowling had never been a walkover, but the element of determination with which she'd managed the launch of her fourth book, even after the stress of having to write it to such an exacting schedule, confirmed that she was now very firmly in charge and would do things her way. Later that autumn she persuaded BBC Radio 4 to broadcast Stephen Fry's unabridged reading of her first novel in one go. It was an extraordinary decision. BBC Radio 4 is very definitely not a station for young people. But then this wasn't a book strictly for young people either. Starting at midday on Boxing Day 2000 the broadcast ran for eight and a half hours. Helen Boaden, then the controller of BBC Radio 4, admitted to being taken aback by the conditions imposed, but eventually agreed. The reading was much talked about that Christmas, but there have been no broadcasts since, perhaps because all of them would have taken a great deal longer.

CHAPTER THIRTEEN

Time off?

W ITH the launch of her fourth novel behind her, Jo thought hard about the way she was working and living. It wasn't that she wanted to give up writing, but she wasn't prepared to continue on the same treadmill which had dictated her every move for the previous four years. She was exhausted.

Just before the publication of her fifth novel in June 2003 she talked about an important decision she'd made to the television journalist, Jeremy Paxman: '. . .when I finished *Goblet of Fire*, I said to – there were only two publishers who had bought the [next] book – and I said to both of them I want to repay my advance. And both of them. . . you could almost hear them having a cardiac arrest on the end of the phone. . . So they said, "Well, how about we do still get the book when you finish it but we don't have a deadline?" So I said okay. So that's how we worked it. So there was no deadline. . . I didn't miss the deadline. Because there was no deadline.'

It was a liberating decision. During those three years Jo Rowling wrote without the tyranny of the annual publication date and she also enjoyed doing some non-Harry Potter writing. She wrote two Harry Potter-related books – *Quidditch Through the Ages* and *Fantastic Beasts and Where to Find Them*, the proceeds from which went to Comic Relief in March 2001. In those books she was able to air some of the vast collection of material she had built up which provided the foundations for the Harry Potter series, but not a word was included that might compromise the integrity of the ongoing story.

Jo was also able to look outwards, away from the sometimes claustrophobic life of a bestselling celebrity author. Towards the end of 2000, she established The Volant Trust (Volant is her mother's maiden name). With the amount of money she was now earning from her books, and possible future revenues from the films, merchandise and related Harry Potter products, she needed to organise a system to deal with the growing number of requests for financial support, and to formalise her finances so that she could target initiatives in which she had a particular interest.

The Trust's priorities are unsurprising. The first reflects her commitment to supporting research into

Multiple Sclerosis, the illness from which her mother died. It was only ten years since Anne Rowling's death. In an article for the journal *Inside MS*, Jo detailed the way in which her mother was misdiagnosed, then given the correct MS diagnosis but virtually no support to deal with its devastating effects.

Jo has spoken often of the effect of losing her mother – she said that the Harry Potter books might have been very different had she not been coping with that loss every day since. The article is well informed and its undoubted bitterness is laced with the author's characteristic dry wit. By the time she wrote it, Jo had discovered that Scotland had a remarkably high incidence of the disease, and that very little had changed in terms of treatment and support. She agreed to become Patron of MS Scotland in 2001 and gave considerable time and money to increase its research, support work and to raise its profile until she resigned the position in 2009.

But her decision to leave the organisation didn't end her commitment to trying to find a cure for the illness. In August 2010 it was announced that J K Rowling had given £10 million to establish the Anne Rowling Regenerative Neurology Clinic in Edinburgh. The clinic will undertake research into a range of degenerative neurological conditions and diseases including Alzheimer's, Parkinson's, Huntingdon's and motor neurone disease.

Time off?

The Volant Trust's second priority is equally unsurprising – to support national and international charities and projects that alleviate social deprivation with a particular emphasis on women's and children's issues. It isn't difficult to work out why Jo Rowling feels so strongly about that.

The Trust's website logo incorporates the word *Volant* written in J K Rowling's handwriting, similar to the well-known signature which characterises the Harry Potter brand, elegantly personalising it. Just as Jo takes a hands-on approach to as much of the business concerning her books as she can, she is closely involved with the work of the Trust.

But that wasn't all she was up to. . .

CHAPTER FOURTEEN

Personal passions and politics

DURING those three years J K Rowling kept herself busy. She became an ambassador for The National Council for One Parent Families, now renamed Gingerbread; she attended the film premiers of *Harry Potter and the Philosopher's Stone* and *Harry Potter and the Chamber of Secrets*; she met her future husband, then a trainee anaesthetist, Neil Murray, married him on Boxing Day in 2001 in the home she bought for her family in Perthshire; and in March 2003 they had a baby boy, David.

The launch of the films marked a watershed for the Harry Potter books. Unless children walked around blindfold, they couldn't help but see images of the actors chosen to play the parts. There was the inevitable outrage from disgruntled readers, but Jo was loyal to the young cast, pronouncing herself delighted with all that was being done to bring the books to the big screen and visiting the set from time to time. She routinely declares that the latest film is her favourite but in 2008 she made a gentle reference to a slight disconnect.

'I very much see the characters that I've imagined, you know. It's been 17 years for me, so the actors are for me a very recent incarnation. I've lived with my imagination for so long.' She has also made it clear that she wants to read the books to her children before they see the films. At her core, and despite her involvement latterly as producer, she is an author.

In many ways the entire story arc of the Harry Potter books is about giving Harry a family. It's a dynamic about which Jo writes with relish. During that period she created a non-fiction family of her own and by all accounts she is delighted with it. Although she and her husband have been meticulous in keeping all three of their children out of the public eye, she has never made any secret of her pleasure in being a mother.

Any mention of the breakdown of her first marriage is always mitigated by her joy in having had Jessica, and she often reminds interviewers that she may be many things, but being a mother is the role she considers the most enjoyable and important. Family life is sacrosanct. We need only look at the dedications in her books to see how important her family is.

However blissful things were at home during that

period, Jo didn't hide away. Her involvement with Gingerbread – she is now the President – gave her a public platform. She gave generously to the organisation but she also used her own hated experience of being on welfare as a single mother to add weight to their work.

In April 2002 she wrote a feisty foreword to 'Like It or Lump It – A Role for the Social Fund in Ending Child Poverty', a report commissioned by the National Council for One Parent Families, Child Poverty Action Group and Family Welfare Association. This wasn't something glitzy – no walk down a red carpet required wearing a designer dress and heels. This was about reality for a sector of society for which Jo believed she could provide a voice.

She focused on practicalities, calling for grants rather than loans for families in need of basic living conditions – beds, cookers and furniture. 'Where does it leave those who have already been forced into debt just to keep their families afloat? Where does it leave those whose incomes are so low they cannot afford to repay a loan?' She wasn't posing these questions simply to make a point. She was using her own experience to make the point. And she continues to use it.

Inevitably Jo was approached to lend her name and support to many causes. She stuck to subjects about which she felt passionate – and angry. In her spirited foreword to *Magic*, a short story anthology for adults published by Bloomsbury to raise funds for the National Council of One Parent Families, Jo challenged readers with some uncomfortable images from her past. She described her possible responses when she was at her most depleted and people asked her, *What do you do?*

'I worry continually, I devote hours to writing a book I doubt will ever be published, I try hard to hold on to the hope that our situation will improve, and when I am not too exhausted to feel strong emotion I am swamped with anger at the portrayals of single mothers by certain politicians and newspapers as feckless teenagers in search of that holy grail, the council flat, when 97% of us have long since left our teens.' If she was going to use her writing to support organisations she cared about, she wasn't going to beat about the bush.

In the anything but poverty-stricken surroundings of the Harvard University Commencement (or Graduation), Jo returned to the subject of poverty in a speech entitled 'The Fringe Benefits of Failure, and the Importance of Imagination'.

'Poverty entails fear and stress and sometimes depression; it means a thousand petty humiliations and hardships. Climbing out of poverty by your own efforts, that is indeed something on which to pride yourself but poverty itself is romanticised only by fools,' she told the Class of 2008.

She also shared memories of working for Amnesty International, of the smuggled letters she had read, accounts of unspeakable horrors in totalitarian regimes in which freedom of speech is not a given, of meeting people terribly damaged by what they had experienced, exiled from their home cultures and families, trying to make a new start in Britain.

These were political points and Jo went out of her way to make them in places where they would be heard and reported. Harvard graduates will go places, professionally and personally, and she would count on them remembering what she'd told them when they got there. She might be the author of bestselling books for children, but there was nothing simplistic about what she said.

In 2008 Jo put her money where her mouth was when she made a donation of £1 million to the Labour Party. She was unafraid of sticking her neck out. Gordon Brown was not a popular Prime Minister at the time, but Jo publicly backed him saying that he had 'consistently prioritised and introduced measures that would save as many children as possible from a life lacking in opportunity or choice.'

And she didn't stop there. In *Time*, the American current affairs magazine, she profiled the then British Prime Minister who had been selected as one of the world's 100 most influential people in 2009. 'I know him as affable, funny and gregarious, a great listener and a kind and loyal friend. These are strange and turbulent times but issues of fairness, equality and protection of the poor have never been more important. I still want Gordon Brown in charge.'

Her unfashionable comments were mocked by some journalists, dismissed as her way of giving a floundering politician friend much needed support. The headline writers had a field day. But nobody was left in any doubt that J K Rowling's communication skills weren't going to be limited to her books. She is angry about social deprivation and exclusion, and that anger led her to take other opportunities to raise those issues in her character-istically feisty, fearless and direct style. Following an article she wrote in *The Times* in April 2010 called The Single Mother's Manifesto, David Cameron will not be expecting a donation to the Conservative Party.

In 2004 J K Rowling revamped www.jkrowling.com, her website, much to the delight of her readers in all six of the languages in which it can be accessed. Although the home page can languish unchanged for long periods, her online fans are quick to seize on the slightest changes and additions that appear and disappear. These include a handwritten sheet from one of the earliest drafts of the first book with a plot possibility which she aband-oned. It's the grubbiest of pieces of paper with scratchy handwriting, blots and coffee stains, but it's priceless.

The website has also proved a useful way of refuting some of the nonsense written about Jo in the press. Her portrayal of the *Daily Prophet*'s Rita Skeeter has caused much debate, but the author refuses to attribute inspiration for the character to a single journalist, insisting that Rita was part of the story long before the press had heard of Harry Potter. Using a virtual rubbish bin full of scrumpled up bits of paper Jo puts the record straight, knowing that her version will be widely reported, re-posted and tweeted.

Those who make assumptions about her personal life receive particularly scathing ripostes. 'Last year several newspapers alleged that my husband had given up work, presumably to sit at home and watch me write. This is one of those stories that make me angry because they hurt my family. . . Neil has NEVER given up work and continues to practise as a doctor in Edinburgh.' She has on occasion asked newspapers to print retractions and she has sued on behalf of her children when she felt their privacy had been compromised. But she would spend her life talking to lawyers if she were to respond to every slight.

Some criticism was less easily rebuffed. When she came under fire from Christian fundamentalists for writing about witches and wizards for children her books were banned by some authorities in America. She has always made it clear that she does not believe in magic of the kind she writes and she obviously doesn't want to be a poster girl for witchcraft or wizardry, but she doesn't want to shatter readers' enjoyment of her books either. It's a fine line to tread. The Harry Potter novels have attracted some high profile critics, including the present Pope who, as Cardinal Ratzinger, described the books as 'subtle seductions'.

Accusations of plagiarism have emerged from time to time. In 2000 Jo and her US publisher Scholastic together with Warner Bros took action against Nancy Stouffer, who had accused her of having lifted ideas from her novels. Stouffer's claim was finally dismissed after appeals in 2006, a decision which now seems so obvious as to be barely worth a footnote, but for Jo the case had been painful and time-consuming. No matter how ridiculous or fraudulent the claim, each necessitates the involvement of lawyers, with all the paperwork that then follows. She has made no secret of her anger at the accusations and the disruption they cause but will never contemplate paying any settlement to her accusers.

Jo has never cited any books that might have inspired her writing although she has always read widely. Most writers have magpie tendencies and she loves books like *Brewer's Dictionary of Phrase and Fable* and *Culpeper's Complete Herbal*, both of which she openly admits to having mined for evocative words and meaningful names. With an honours degree in Classics it is inevitable that she would draw on a wide range of the ancient mythologies with which she is familiar.

In an interview with the American magazine *Newsweek* in June 2003 she gave a revealing answer to a question about whether her adopted home city influenced her writing. 'I could go anywhere in the world and produce it word for word the same. But I do think being British is very important. Because we do have a motley, mongrel folklore here, and I was interested in it and collected it. And then I got the idea for Harry.'

In 2008, J K Rowling travelled to New York to ensure that on this occasion her copyright was not infringed by a planned guide to her books – *The Harry Potter Lexicon,* by Steve Vander Ark. She, along with Warner Bros., had filed a suit against the publisher of the guide. The experience was upsetting and the press was in part uncharacteristically unsympathetic. It looked to some, who had not fully understood the facts or the implications for creative people in general, like a David and Goliath-type tussle, the multi-millionaire author and the Hollywood studio stomping on the dreams of one of her most devoted fans. Steve had run the highly regarded Harry Potter Lexicon website and she had publicly praised it. The court's decision was that the guide infringed rights as it took huge chunks of Jo's work and reproduced them as if they had been written by Steve and not Jo. It was later agreed that there could be a published Lexicon from Steve as long as the contents were altered to avoid quoting from the books themselves and where quotes were taken, that Jo be credited as the author of the words and not Steve. The revised version – *The Lexicon* – was published in 2009.

The issue of copyright and the rights to the books and characters owned by Warner Bros. have led to a number of altercations with fan websites and certain URL owners were asked to transfer ownership to them (eg www.harrypotterguide.com) whilst allowing them to carry on using the URL. Schools have been confused as to why they aren't given permission to stage end of term productions of Harry Potter stories. There are guidelines issued by Warner Bros for Harry Potter-themed events but they don't ask for the fictional character to be removed. These exchanges can be uncomfortable and sometimes attract negative press.

It is hard for lay people to comprehend the legal intricacies of copyright. Harry Potter character names and any other names, including those of shops or sweets used in the books are trademarks belonging to Warner Bros. Entertainment Inc., who also own the copyright. J K Rowling owns the copyright to all Harry Potter publishing. The implications of the deal J K Rowling struck with Warner Bros. were and are profound. Business interests the world over rely on its stability.

CHAPTER FIFTEEN

Onwards, upwards and outwards

HARRY Potter and the Order of the Phoenix went on sale at midnight on June 21st, 2003. Once again, all kinds of arrangements and security had been put in place to ensure that there was not a single copy available before the allotted time. No detail of the plot – other than those tantalisingly revealed in advance by the author herself – was to be made public. Bookshops, often lavishly decorated, opened specially, ushering in readers of all ages, many dressed up for the occasion.

I joined the line on Edinburgh's Princes Street outside Waterstone's East End branch as I'd been asked to review the book for a newspaper with a delivery deadline for the following afternoon. Along at the West End branch, an unpublicised signing was taking place with the author herself. I had been underwhelmed by the prospect of heading into town so late at night. I'd stocked up on strong coffee for the task ahead but the general exuberance of the Harry Potter devotees and the booksellers that night meant that I went home energised and ready for it. I put the book down about 6am, cross-eyed and exhausted. I love the books although I am not a Harry Potter obsessive – I'm not that kind of a reader – but even so, I thoroughly enjoyed returning to the world of the now very adolescent boy wizard.

On June 26th, I went to the Albert Hall in London with thousands of others for an event that was to be webcast throughout the world. Jo was to read from the new book, and she was to be interviewed, again, by Stephen Fry.

The atmosphere was electric. Her progression up the red carpet, signing books as she went, was shown on huge screens set up on stage via which questions would be posed by readers in other parts of the world. It was an elaborate production. Stephen Fry whipped the audience into a frenzy to ensure ear-splitting cheering to welcome the main act on stage. Jo Rowling looked pleased but, as usual, slightly embarrassed by the razzmatazz of it all.

'I'm not a natural ta-da kind of person,' she once said of her public appearances. 'I get all uptight about having to do that sort of stuff and I feel like a prat.' She was at her most relaxed when readers put her on the spot. 'Harry saw his parents die so why hasn't he been able to see the Thestrals before?' asked one. 'If you looked into the mirror of Erised what do you think you would see?' asked another.

Once that part of the event was over Jo set up the reading from the new book, giving us a page reference so that we might read along with her. The reading was matter of fact. You could have heard a pin drop through-out. The cheers that followed her departure echoed round the cavernous venue.

The event had been beamed to readers all over the world. Jo had avoided Googling Harry Potter or herself until some time in 2002 and although she was aware of online activity, she had been blown away by what she found. In her foreword to *Harry, A History* by super-fan and web-mistress of the Leaky Cauldron Website, Melissa Anelli, Jo wrote, 'I sat and read editorials, predictions, theories that ranged from strange to wild to perfectly accurate. I was, frankly, stunned. . . and I remain stunned.' She was particularly struck by the 'shippers' – groups of readers who championed one relationship (Harry/Hermione or Ron/Hermione) over another.

Melissa's book details the terrific energy, creativity, ingenuity and camaraderie of the Harry Potter web communities. Authors have always had fan clubs, and fan letters are common, but the sophisticated online presence focussing on Harry Potter is enormous. Traditional fan clubs relied on publishers and authors to generate information, distributing it in magazines and newsletters. Jo needed to do nothing to keep her fan sites happy – they generate information all for themselves. The amount of time Harry Potter readers must spend staring at screens the world over doesn't bear thinking about. Online conversations, debates, arguments and suggestions rattle on 24/7.

Fan fiction was another huge part of the Harry Potter phenomenon. Not all authors like it, because their characters are taken over by other writers, thrown into situations which may be bizarre, outrageous or downright unsuitable. It was an area of her following that Jo couldn't ignore. On her behalf, her literary agent explained that she was 'very flattered' but that Jo's 'concern would be to make sure that it remains a non-commercial activity to ensure fans are not exploited and it is not being published in the strict sense of traditional print publishing.' The warning was clear, if gentle.

Harry Potter and the Order of the Phoenix broke the previous sales figures for the launch weekend. The BBC reported sales of 1,777,000 in the UK and over 5 million copies in America. Retailers were reeling from the demand. The supermarket chain Sainsbury reported double the expected sales and Tesco reckoned that they had sold 220 copies every minute on launch day. Amazon, the internet retailer, announced that it had taken orders for 1.3 million copies of the book globally. Copies were even selling well in countries for which English is not the first language. The strict embargo on the book's availability prior to publication day meant that the international team of translators of the Harry Potter books wouldn't be able to start on their work until then either. Foreign publishers – Harry Potter had by then been translated into 55 languages – would have to wait.

The intensity of feeling about the Harry Potter books is the reason why J K Rowling felt it was so important to keep to the midnight launch. The fans wanted a part in a big international event and the only way to involve them was to give them an international event. The need for secrecy and security was again paramount. Bookshops signed agreements that detailed exactly what they were and weren't allowed to do with their orders, exactly what the rules were on storing and opening the boxes of stock. Bloomsbury employees were, to all intents and purposes, gagged. The element of secrecy was compounded by the ambitious logistics. The pressure on the sales teams, the distribution networks and the retailers was extraordinary.

CHAPTER SIXTEEN

Battle of the bookshops

THE supermarkets had been delighted by sales, and they wanted to capitalise on that success in time for the next launch. This put the bookselling operation in a whole new light. To understand the impact of the supermarkets' interest, it is useful to know a bit about how books are usually sold.

Bookshops buy stock from publishers at a discount and depending on the size of the discount, they may sell certain books at a reduced price. Most online retailers offer a discount of some kind or other while earthbound bookshops offer Buy-One-Get-One-Free or Three-for-the-Price-of-Two promotions. Books in these promotions are prominently displayed on tables or face out in displays and so they get noticed. Books that aren't in promotions have usually been supplied at a smaller discount although that doesn't mean they are in any way inferior.

In the case of the next Harry Potter novel, the volume of sales anticipated by the supermarkets, chain booksellers, independent bookshops and online retailers was vast. How would they ensure that customers came to them and not their competitors for their copies? The most obvious incentive is price, and although Blooms-bury defended their discounting structure against accusations of unfairness, it would be daft to pretend that those placing the biggest orders would not have received the biggest discounts. The bigger the discounts, the lower the price shops could afford to charge for the book.

Small independent bookshops were in a difficult position. They couldn't afford to order in quantities that would attract big discounts – so they couldn't reduce the price of the book as much as their large competitors. Some specialist children's booksellers believed that it was their hard work and support in the early days that had given Harry Potter such a good start. Now they might miss out on the rewards. They could only hope that their customers would remain loyal and resist the temptations of the local supermarket.

However miffed, no bookseller of any size would have dared open on publication day without copies of the new book for sale. Each had to decide at what price they could afford to sell the book. They wouldn't want to be undercut by another retailer, but they wouldn't want to make a loss either, by discounting too deeply.

It was a question of which retailer blinked first. Some offered incentives – a free *Dragonology* book if an advance order was placed. Others invited customers to launch parties. Some supermarkets planned to sell the book as a loss leader, believing that the slight loss on each copy would be justified by the increased number of customers they would attract into their stores.

Janet Smyth had met Jo Rowling in the early days of her career, taking her into a couple of Edinburgh primary schools as part of the Readiscovery project she ran. Now she was the owner of a small children's bookshop in Linlithgow in West Lothian, and she ordered enough copies to cover all her customer pre-orders and a modest number of shelf copies.

'So many people turned up that had never visited the shop before or since to get a copy,' Janet says, 'it sold through by mid morning on the launch day. Because the book immediately went into reprint the day it was published the only way to get copies – and get them fast – was to buy from the nearest supermarket. These copies were actually cheaper than we could buy them from Bloomsbury. We just de-stickered them and sold them at a modest discount. I have heard tales of other independent bookshops getting all their stock in this way – refusing to order any direct from the publisher or wholesaler. The whole thing was fairly mad but the pressure from kids to have the books the moment they were legally available was very hard to resist. If we hadn't opened the shop at midnight, or if we hadn't stocked the book simply because we couldn't have afforded to, we would have looked like losers. We ended up having a really good day. Our turnover was great but the profit margin was non-existent.'

Jo Rowling was aware of the problem. She posted a message on her website just prior to the publication of the final Harry Potter novel thanking 'booksellers everywhere but particularly in the UK, because they were crucial to Harry's initial success which was built, not on clever marketing, but on word-of-mouth recommend-ations. . . Harry has become hard work for booksellers in later days, with embargoes and crowds making everything much more fraught, and much less intimate than it used to be (though many throw themselves into the spirit of midnight openings); I am deeply grateful.'

CHAPTER SEVENTEEN

And they all lived. . .

A SPECIAL event was staged at the Edinburgh International Book Festival on August 15th, 2004. The organisers knew better than to include it in the programme. That would have caused mayhem. Instead they announced the event with a month to go, offering tickets in a ballot. As soon as the news was out, requests for tickets were emailed in from all over the world.

I introduced Jo at the event – inasmuch as she needed any introduction. My main responsibility was to make sure it ended at the correct time, making me the most unpopular person in the tent. Perhaps because it wasn't a launch year Jo was particularly relaxed. The Q&A that followed her reading had the intensity of a Mastermind final, except that there was more laughter. The only hesitation was when she needed to make sure she wasn't giving anything away. Otherwise she was in sparkling form, funny, dry and teasing, dropping little hints about what the next book might bring, wondering why she'd never been asked certain questions about the plot.

Harry Potter and the Half-Blood Prince was published eleven months later at midnight on July 16th, 2005, six months after the birth of Jo's second daughter, Mackenzie. This time the launch was held at Edinburgh Castle, a 10-minute drive from J K Rowling's home. Young journalists were flown from all over the world for a special press conference in which they were each allowed to ask a single question. I stood on the chilly Castle Esplanade alongside crowds of people hoping to catch a glimpse of the world famous author. My deadline was 4pm the following afternoon so once again, picking up my review copy, it was home to a pot of coffee and a night of reading. Once again I wasn't disappointed.

Of course, not all the newspaper reviews were positive, and as so often happens, popularity can breed contempt. 'The prose is sometimes risibly clichéd,' observes one while another decides, 'This is the kind of prose that reasonably intelligent nine-year-olds consider pretty hot stuff, if they're producing it themselves. . .' Some felt that the books should have been more tightly edited, or that J K Rowling wasn't being edited at all. But for young readers, length was not an issue. It was the wait for the next book that caused the problems.

And they all lived. . .

Harry Potter and the Deathly Hallows, the seventh and final novel, was published at midnight on July 21st, 2007, bringing to a conclusion the story that had gripped millions of readers all over the world. Fifteen million copies were sold in 24 hours. It was another remarkable publishing feat, shrouded in secrecy. Although there were a few creaks in the operation, given its scale, they were minimal. In America a Braille edition was published simultaneously. Scholastic Inc. had released the book two weeks early to the National Braille Press, where staff worked intensively in secret to transcribe it in time for the official launch date. Bloomsbury published the hardback for children, the hardback for adults, the unabridged CD for children, the same for adults, and a large print hardback for people with limited vision – all at the same time. At the precise moment these went on sale in bookshops up and down Britain, the author was seated in front of a hall full of 2000 children in London's Natural History Museum. She acknowledged the cheers, opened the book and began to read.

Launch events and celebrations were taking place throughout the UK. Janet Smyth had organised her final Harry Potter launch event – a Midnight Ceilidh – which was so successful that she found herself in the early hours of the morning heading once again to the local 24-hour supermarket to replenish her stock. 'I've often wondered why the most anticipated book in the world wasn't sold at full price – it's the one book everybody would have forked out for without giving it a second thought,' she says.

During the year leading up to the final publication date, Jo had agreed to take part in a television documentary made by the writer and broadcaster James Runcie, called 'J K Rowling – A Year in her Life'. This was quite a risk for somebody who had protected her privacy so carefully. The programme shows her at home, working, at meetings, baking a birthday cake, travelling on a private jet provided by Bloomsbury to take her and her husband to London for the launch of the book, at a film premiere, working through letters with her PA, Fiddy – all the activities which now fill her life.

James Runcie was aware that his subject was no pushover. 'I had to be very careful about what I said and what I did. She's very protected and I knew that if I made one false move the door would close,' he said. He had briefly wondered whether it would be appropriate for a millionaire author to take a budget flight to visit her childhood home near Exeter but she proved happy to do so. There is footage of Jo at a meeting in an Edinburgh hotel with the team of theme park designers who came all the way from Florida to discuss their plans. James Runcie seems excited to see the Harry Potter phenomenon at such close range. But he sees it for what it is. At one point he says, 'I think it must be quite odd to be J K

Rowling. Half of her life seems almost normal while the other half seems completely mad.'

Jo is filmed on the night of the launch of her seventh novel being driven to the Natural History Museum in London. She knows what's ahead. In an earlier clip of a planning meeting for the event, one of her publicists calmly announced, 'Jo's agreed to sign for eight hours.' She signed 1700 books that night.

The publication of *Harry Potter and the Deathly Hallows* brought to an end the story Jo Rowling had planned so meticulously. The final chapter, written many years earlier in which we discover how the future unfolded for Harry, Ron and Hermione finally saw the light of day with some modifications, delighting or dismaying the 'shippers'. She had finished the novel the previous January in a room, now renamed The J K Rowling Suite, in Edinburgh's Balmoral Hotel, where the bust of Hermes on which she recorded the achievement in felt pen is now displayed in a glass case.

But J K Rowling was not finished. She had further Harry Potter tales to tell.

In January 2006 Jo had become involved with the Children's High Level Group, a charity committed to improving child welfare and protection, particularly in Eastern Europe. She travelled to Bucharest in Romania to mark the charity's launch alongside Baroness Emma

Nicholson who had already been working to reduce the number of Romanian children living in care institutions. Jo posted the news on her website, admitting that when she'd first seen a mention of the plight of the institution-alised children in a newspaper she had found the accompanying photograph so disturbing that she'd turned it over. Such candour combined with her high media profile is the perfect combination for a hard-hitting charity.

J K Rowling's philanthropy is not only about signing large cheques, it's also about being a magnet for other large cheques. Her initial visit to Bucharest was to attend a fund-raising dinner. People pay significant amounts of money for the honour of sitting in the same room as the internationally renowned author.

The Tales of Beedle the Bard are mentioned in *Harry Potter and the Deathly Hallows*, a book of wizarding fairy tales that Dumbledore leaves to Hermione. In November 2007 on her website J K Rowling announced that she had made seven copies – written and illustrated by hand, bound in leather and decorated in silver and semi-precious stones. Six of them would be given as thank yous to the people whom she described as having been 'most closely involved with Harry Potter over the years'. The seventh was to be auctioned at Sotheby's in London with the proceeds going to The Children's High Level Group. When that auction took place, the book fetched £1.95 million.

And they all lived. . .

In 2010 J K Rowling became Chair of Lumos, the charity that evolved from The Children's High Level Group. Its byline is 'working to transform the lives of disadvantaged children' and its work remains largely focused in Eastern Europe, except Romania. Royalties from the published edition of *The Tales of Beedle the Bard* went to support the work of the Children's High Level Group, and now Lumos.

It must seem extraordinary, given her circumstances in the mid 1990s, to be able to give financial aid to the extent that J K Rowling now can. But she is a hands-on philanthropist, and won't simply provide the introduction to the annual report – she'll read it with a pencil at the ready. In 2007 J K Rowling awarded one of her Fan Site Awards to the Harry Potter Alliance and it is not hard to see why. 'The Harry Potter Alliance fights the Dark Arts in the real world by using parallels from Harry Potter. We work for human rights, equality and a better world just as Harry and his friends did throughout the books.' The HPA offers a most engaging outward-looking alternative to the other crammed fan-sites. Members campaign for fairtrade chocolate to be used in all Harry Potter-related sweets alongside appeals for money to provide aid for Haiti. It's just another remarkable manifestation of the impact the Harry Potter stories have made on their readers' lives.

CHAPTER EIGHTEEN

And finally. . .

JAMES Runcie is right. J K Rowling's is an odd life. Her signature is trademarked, her face has been created in Lego, she was recreated as a one-off Barbie doll, she receives upwards of 75,000 letters every year, Oprah Winfrey came all the way to Edinburgh to interview her (without the press picking up on either the visit or the interview), she was awarded the first ever Hans Christian Andersen Literature Award, she was the second person (after Ian Rankin) to be given the Edinburgh Award which led to her handprints being immortalised in Caithness stone, she has a gold Blue Peter badge, she read aloud to Michelle Obama in London's Royal Opera House and sat next to Barack Obama that evening at dinner in 10 Downing Street, she has honorary doctorates from universities throughout Britain, she was named a *Chevalier de l'Ordre de la Légion d'Honneur*, she has an OBE, she is a Patron of Scotland's Maggie Centres for cancer care, she appears regularly on lists of the most powerful, the richest, the most influential, and she is a mother of three children with everything that entails. Normality? Madness?

The author herself is more straightforward. 'I'm a born trier,' she told James Runcie, and when he asked how she would like to be remembered she replied, 'Somebody who did the best she could with the talent she had.'

Back to those Harvard graduates in the summer of 2008. . .

> 'If you choose to use your status and influence to raise your voice on behalf of those who have no voice; if you choose to identify not only with the powerful, but with the powerless; if you retain the ability to imagine yourself into the lives of those who do not have your advantages, then it will not only be your proud families who celebrate your existence, but thousands and millions of people whose reality you have helped change. We do not need magic to change the world, we carry all the power we need inside ourselves already: we have the power to imagine better.'

That's an inspiring way with which to end a speech for young people about to graduate from one of the world's top universities, but it could also be read as an agreement that J K Rowling has made with herself, a way of dealing with what has happened to her.

Oprah Winfrey asked Jo what difference money had made in her life. She enjoyed dressing better, she said, and she could plan a family holiday without worrying about its cost. Her passion for designer shoes is also well known. But wealth brings responsibilities alongside privilege and perks. It is as a philanthropist that she now operates, using her wealth to generate further funds for causes in which she has a personal passionate interest, using her public profile, and the inevitable allure of the super-rich and super-successful to drum up support, using her powers of communication to look people in the eye and tell them that life for many people in the world is simply not fair.

Jo Rowling has had more fictional and real choices to make than most of us since 1997. What if she hadn't taken the plunge and written the book? What if it hadn't landed on the desks it subsequently did? What if it hadn't caught the imagination of children everywhere? What if she hadn't chosen Warner Bros.? What if she'd given up after *Harry Potter and the Goblet of Fire*?

Although she's in no doubt that she will continue to write, Jo seems unsure about whether she'll ever revisit the world she created in the Harry Potter novels except in her imagination. In some interviews she's adamant she won't and in others she won't be drawn.

I'm more certain.

And finally. . .

Towards the end of the documentary 'J K Rowling, A Year in her Life' she is filmed plotting out Harry Potter's family tree on a piece of paper. There's not a moment's hesitation as she scribbles down full names, marries them off, lists their offspring and godparents' names, all the time providing a running commentary for the benefit of the programme maker.

Harry and Ginny have three children, she tells him – *James Sirius, Albus Severus and Lily Luna*. As she writes the middle child's name she says quickly, 'Albus Severus, who's the one I'm most interested in. . .'

What if. . . ?

BIBLIOGRAPHY

There is so much information and footage online about the Harry Potter phenomenon – hours, days, weeks go by once you start clicking through the pages, but those I found most useful were:

www.accio-quote.org

www.bbc.co.uk

www.hp-lexicon.org

www.jkrfan.com

www.jkrowling.com

www.mugglenet.com

www.the-leaky-cauldron.org

Harry, A History by Melissa Anelli (Pocket Books, 2008)

An Interview with J K Rowling by J K Rowling and Lindsey Fraser (Mammoth, 2000)

Harry Potter and the Philosopher's Stone J K Rowling (Bloomsbury, 1997)

Harry Potter and the Chamber of Secrets J K Rowling (Bloomsbury, 1998)

Harry Potter and the Prisoner of Azkaban J K Rowling (Bloomsbury, 1999)

Harry Potter and the Goblet of Fire J K Rowling (Bloomsbury, 2000)

Fantastic Beasts and Where to Find Them J K Rowling (Bloomsbury, 2001)

Quidditch Through the Ages J K Rowling (Bloomsbury, 2001)

Harry Potter and the Order of the Phoenix J K Rowling (Bloomsbury, 2003)

Harry Potter and the Half-Blood Prince J K Rowling (Bloomsbury, 2005)

Harry Potter and the Deathly Hallows J K Rowling (Bloomsbury, 2007)

Tales of Beedle the Bard J K Rowling (published by Lumos in association with Bloomsbury Publishing plc, 2008)